JOURNAL OF CAMUS STUDIES
2014

JOURNAL OF CAMUS STUDIES
2014

General Editor
Peter Francev

Camus Society
2014

Journal of Camus Studies 2014

General Editor: Peter Francev
Book Reviews Editor: Eric B. Berg
Book Design: Helen Lea
Cover Design: Simon Lea

The purpose of the *Journal of Camus Studies* is to further understanding of the work and thought of Albert Camus.

The *Journal of Camus Studies* is a publication of the Albert Camus Society. The material contained in this journal represents the opinions of the authors and not necessarily those of the Albert Camus Society or anyone affiliated with the society.

First Printing: 2014

www.camus-society.com
www.camus-us.com

ISBN: 978-1-326-09098-2

CONTENTS

INTRODUCTION

Since 2009, the *Journal of Camus Studies* (formerly, *The Journal of the Albert Camus Society UK*) has been *the* source for the latest studies and perspectives in Camus scholarship. Once again, before you, is a thorough collection of scintillating essays from Camus scholars the world over. Of course, producing a fine journal takes the dedicated work of several individuals, namely: Simon and Helen Lea, Matthew Bowker, and the anonymous reviews committee members, whose fine eye helps produce such fine academic contributions. The 2015 *Journal of Camus Studies* will be out in early spring 2015 and will contain the 2014 conference essays. It is with great enthusiasm that I hope you enjoy this and future journals. Without your support, none of this would be possible. Thank you.

Peter Francev
Editor, *Journal of Camus Studies*
President of the Albert Camus Society US

Queer Subversions: Unmappable Bodies in Albert Camus's *The Stranger*

by Ceylan Ceyhun Arslan

Albert Camus writes in his preface to the American university edition of *The Stranger*: "[Meursault] is foreign to the society in which he lives; he wanders, on the fringe, in the suburbs of private, solitary, sensual life" ("Preface," 336). Camus emphasizes that Meursault's sensuality constitutes a peripheral space. Furthermore, Meursault never stays still in this space, but he instead constantly "wanders." This ceaseless movement that takes place on the fringes of society echoes Sedgwick's definition of the queer: "Queer is a continuing moment, movement, motive—recurrent, eddying, *troublant*" (*Tendencies* xii). Based on this generic definition, I claim that Camus here delineates a queer Meursault. Meursault's queerness becomes conspicuous particularly when Meursault expresses a wish to kiss a man for the first time in his life during the court trial. I designate this moment as a point of departure for a queer reading and argue that the body constitutes a nebulous and even unmappable territory in *The Stranger*. The portrayal of the body in the novel counteracts its normative conceptualizations as a coherent, immotile, and demarcated entity. This portrayal instead substantiates Elizabeth Grosz's depiction of the body in *Volatile Bodies: Toward a Corporeal Feminism* as "discontinuous, nontotalizable series of processes, organs, flows, energies, corporeal substances and incorporeal events, speeds and durations" (164).

   In the first section of this article, I claim that Meursault's wish to kiss a man is queer not just because it represents an articulation of same-sex affinity. It also does not hinge upon a rigidly systematized mapping of Céleste's body that posits it as a closed entity. Instead, Meursault has a shimmering vision, which corresponds to Grosz's depiction of the body as a series of flows. Yet Meursault's wish to a kiss a man is not the sole queer instant that seeps into an otherwise perfectly heteronormative world. Marie, with whom Meursault started to have a relationship one day after his mother's funeral, also undermines solid, stabilized, and "nonqueer" mappings of the body during moments of intimacy.

The second section demonstrates that the sun and the Arab nurse represent elements which remind Meursault that he can never attain a disembodied existence that allows him to scrupulously map its objects of gaze. As a result, Meursault never remains shielded from his environs that dissolve solid boundaries. His inability to attain total disembodiment demonstrates that Meursault can never lead a life of uninterrupted normativity. Such a reading promises reinvigorating insights about the role of the sun and the Arab nurse that the Camus scholarship has not explored before. Abstract Euro-American philosophical debates provided the ground for discussion on the sun motif among critics, which disassociates the sun from its ecological milieu that forces Meursault to confront his corporeality. At the same time, postcolonial readings exclusively focus on the silence and powerlessness of Arabs, which glosses over the Arab nurse's disorienting and stalwart role in shaping Meursault's mindset. Meursault's gaze is unable to anatomize the Arab nurse's body; in fact, the sun's omnipresent gaze seems to anatomize Meursault's body. Thus, the prominent postcolonial readings in which the body of the colonized becomes subject to the scrupulous mapping of the colonizer cannot encapsulate the queer dynamics prevalent in *The Stranger*. Even Meursault's decapitation cannot put an end to the *troublant*, queer movements that characterize the novel.

I

When Céleste gives a witness testimony during the trial in *The Stranger*, we read a section that invites a queer reading:

> [Céleste] was asked ... what he thought of me, and he
> answered that I was a man; what he meant by that, and he
> stated that everybody knew what that meant; if he had
> noticed that I was ever withdrawn, and all he would admit
> was that I didn't speak unless I had something to say. The
> prosecutor asked him if I kept up with my bill. Céleste
> laughed and said, "Between us those were just details." . . .
> And as if he had reached the end of both his knowledge and
> his goodwill, Céleste then turned toward me. It looked to
> me as if his eyes were glistening and his lips were
> trembling. He seemed to be asking me what else he could
> do. I said nothing; I made no gesture of any kind, but it was
> the first time in my life I ever wanted to kiss a man. (92–93)

Meursault becomes overtly identified with a particular gender category—"man." The judge does not find this identification clear, and hence asks Céleste "what he mean[s] by that." Yet Céleste assumes that what he means by "man" should be crystal clear to everyone and feels no need to elaborate on its definition. Confronting a judge who wants to carve out every detail about Meursault's life, Céleste holds back information, as "all he would admit" is Meursault's reticent demeanor. Laughing, he unhesitatingly and daringly asserts to the audience that his relationship with Meursault entails details that he will not share with others, especially in a courtroom full of people voracious to diligently map Meursault.

At a fleeting moment, insulated from the rest of the overwhelming crowd in the court, Meursault concentrates on and interprets carefully Céleste's body language, while also letting us know that no one at the courtroom could read his motives, as he "sa[ys] nothing" and "[makes] no gesture of any kind." This is an open declaration to the reader: The relationship between Céleste and Meursault has many facets that cannot be verbalized to people in the courtroom, however adamant they are in meticulously carving out details about Meursault's life.

"But," Meursault declares, a momentous moment during his narrative. Until then, Meursault displayed his narrative power to remain illegible. Yet he now articulates a wish enacted by his reading of Céleste's body: "But it was the first time in my life I ever wanted to kiss a man." That Meursault wants something is subversive in itself, since he otherwise remains tenaciously indifferent to the world, which rarely incites a strong desire within him.

Furthermore, Meursault's wish to kiss a man represents a countermove against the tendency to shoehorn one into a gender category that one assumes to have the same, solid, and diaphanous meaning for everyone. If Céleste defines "the Man," Meursault wants to kiss "a man." Till this moment, Meursault only wanted to kiss Marie. Now demarcated as a man, Meursault wants to kiss *a* man, *any* man, and not specifically Céleste. What first seems a delimiting, imposing and even asphyxiating move— to forcefully endow someone with a gender category and define that person based on that identity ("he is a man")— becomes instantaneously retorted by an articulation of a desire that lacks a clear-cut direction ("I want to kiss a man"). This lack of clarity contrasts with Céleste's bold certainty.

This wish invites a queer reading of the novel not necessarily because it is steered toward a man. The key phrase here is "as if": Meursault has a shimmering, blurry vision of Céleste's body when we read, "as if [Céleste's] eyes were glistening and his lips were trembling." The ambiguity captured in the phrase "as if" reflects his uncertainty. Also note the repeated movement implicated by the word "trembling." This flickering vision leads Meursault to articulate a wish that I consider queer. Herein lies a moment in which Meursault's desire does not hinge upon a stable and meticulous mapping of the body.

The courtroom is not the first place in which Meursault is endowed with a gender category. Before the court scene, his friend, Raymond, identifies Meursault as a man in two instances:

> Then he told me that as a matter of fact he wanted to ask my advice about the whole business, because I was a man, I knew about things, I could help him out, and then we'd be pals. I didn't say anything, and he asked me again if I wanted to be pals. (29, emphasis added)

> I got up. Raymond gave me a very firm handshake and said that men always understand each other. I left his room, closing the door behind me, and paused for a minute in the dark, on the landing. (33, emphasis added)

Meursault's immediate reactions could be silent, stalwart refusals to concur with these identifications: He does not say anything or leaves the room the moment Raymond classifies Meursault as a man. Never once, in fact, Meursault self-identifies as a man. Speaking of his tortuous days at the prison, Meursault notes, "I was tormented by my desire for a woman. It was only natural; I was young" (77). It was natural for Meursault to desire a woman, not because he is a man, but instead because he is young.

Why does Meursault never self-identify as a man? The answer lies in the following statement he gave during the interrogation: "Nevertheless I answered that I had pretty much lost the habit of analyzing myself" (65). Meursault rarely delves into deep self-reflection. This enacts a style that resists orchestrating disparate facts under a coherent narrative which the beginning of the novel beautifully epitomizes: "Maman died today. Or yesterday maybe, I don't know. I got a telegram from the home: 'Mother deceased. Funeral tomorrow. Faithfully yours.' That doesn't mean anything. Maybe it was yesterday" (3).

His aversion to self-reflection makes Meursault the epitomic pariah of a society that relies too much on subjecting people to identity categories. In the courtroom, Meursault always has difficulty in acquiescing to the identity of the criminal: "I was about to say that that was precisely because they were criminals. But then I realized that I was one too. It was an idea that I couldn't get used to" (69–70). Right before the execution, he says, "I had lived my life one way and I could just as well have lived it another. I had done this and I hadn't done that. I hadn't done this thing but I had done another. And so?" (121). Meursault's formulaic statement exposes the fictiveness of identity categories—everyone after all has the same story: doing certain things while not doing others. It is in his resilience to fit into demarcated identities that we should seek the difficulty of shoehorning Meursault into a category of gender and sexuality, which forms coherent narratives of desire and hence stabilizes mappings of the body.

Even though Meursault subverts monolithic categorizations in both sections of the novel, he expresses a wish to kiss a man for the first time ever at part II. This desire thus marks the transformation that occurs in Meursault, acutely crystallized by David Carroll in

Albert Camus the Algerian: "A crucial reversal occurs in the second part of the novel: Meursault's political condition and social identity are radically transformed after his arrest. No longer ignored as an inconsequential French clerk . . . . Meursault loses his privileged place as a French citizen in colonial society and over the course of the second half of the novel is increasingly identified with and put in the place of the colonized Arab, the anonymous, indigenous Other" (31–32). Meursault attains a central status in the mania of mapping that spreads through the entire court and becomes the shared object of stigmatization in part II: "Then [the clerk] looked at me without saying anything, leaned forward rather abruptly, and said very quickly, 'What interests me is you'" (66). We also read, "It took some doing on my part to understand that I was the cause of all the excitement" (83). This incessant mapping sometimes deprives Meursault of the agency to speak when the lawyer adopts Meursault's identity during the defense: "At one point, tough, I listened, because [the lawyer] was saying, 'It is true that I killed a man.' He went on like that, saying 'I' whenever he was speaking about me. I was completely taken aback" (103).

In part I, however, Meursault often asserts an agency to map during moments of physical intimacy with Marie, as his narrative partitions Marie's body into rigidly defined fragments and creates an ossified corporeal cartography of her. Focusing on the motif of kissing in the novel sheds light upon the convoluted terrain of their relationship. I already analyzed the ramifications of Meursault's desire to kiss a man in part II, which opens up a new vista for a queer reading of the novel. In part I, Meursault's kisses form hegemony over Marie's body that brims with undermining potentials. Here, Meursault employs a strong will to diligently map Marie. But Marie's acts of physical intimacy subvert this will.

In Meursault's narrative lens, Marie's body becomes concretized — never ambiguous, always meticulously mapped. Here are two segments wherein Camus uses the word "kiss" in Part I:

> I helped her onto a float and as I did, I brushed against her breasts. I was still in the water when she was already lying flat on her stomach on the float. She turned toward me. Her hair was in her eyes and she was laughing. I hoisted myself

> up next to her. It was nice, and, sort of joking around, I let my head fall back and rest on her stomach. She didn't say anything so I left it there. . . . She had her leg pressed against mine. I was fondling her breasts. Toward the end of the show, I gave her a kiss. (19–20)

> I wanted her so bad when I saw her in that pretty red-and-white striped dress and leather sandals. You could make out the shape of her firm breasts, and her tan made her face look like a flower. . . . Then Marie saw over to me and pressed herself against me in the water. She put her lips on mine. Her tongue cooled my lips and we tumbled in the waves for a moment.
> When we'd gotten dressed again on the beach, Marie looked at me with her eyes sparkling. I kissed her. We didn't say anything more from that point on. (34–35)

Note that, unlike in part II, Meursault never says he *wants* to kiss Marie. His kisses seem like automatic responses, reflexes that arise from his narrative perspective, which dissects Marie into demarcated corporeal segments—eyes, lips, legs, face, tongue, stomach, and breasts. The narrator's frequent use of "I" attests that Meursault has the upper hand in this form of hegemonic mapping, while Marie remains voiceless, her corporeal contours chiseled solely by Meursault's gaze.

Here, one sees no trace of the ambiguity that characterizes what transpired between Céleste and Meursault in the courtroom, exemplified by the phrase "as if his eyes were glistening." Instead, we observe Meursault's curt and declarative sentences when he speaks about Marie's body, and his unquestioning, bold confidence when he describes her body, as he says, "Marie looked at me with her eyes sparkling." His kiss has a silencing, censoring effect, since they "didn't say anything more from that point on."

At first, nothing seems queer between Meursault and Marie. Yet Marie is a much more interesting character than a mold ready to be sculpted by Meursault. To bring forth the subversion that Marie, I requote the following phrase: "Then Marie saw over to me and pressed herself against me in the water. She put her lips on mine" (34–35). Pay attention to the disparity between these two phrases:

"She put her lips on mine" and "I kissed her." The latter covers up the former's corporeality and forcefulness that one can legitimately read as intrusive and even offensive. Furthermore, the former, unlike the latter, could sound unsettling and threatening to Meursault, as we read during another moment of intimacy: "Then, seeing me so confused, she laughed again and she moved toward me with her whole body to offer me her lips" (42– 43).

Unlike Meursault, Marie never "kisses." Instead, at these moments, she "gives," "puts," or "offers" her lips. Thus, lips stand for an object of exchange. The menacing and combative character of this exchange becomes conspicuous especially when Marie "throw[s] a kiss" at Meursault (76) or when "Marie [swims] over to [Meursault] and [presses] herself against [him] in the water" (34). Marie never remains as a frozen object that Meursault could easily sculpt into clearly defined body segments; she, seeing Meursault confused, laughs, and "move[s] . . . with her whole body," displaying her subversive agency to put a seal on Meursault—putting her lips on his. Meursault's body cannot remain insulated from the circuit of exchanges that characterizes their relationship, which also implicitly points to the perpetual fluidity, instability of the body—after all, once body fragments enter a constant flux of exchanges, they leave the stable domain of one's absolute possession. Thus, the boundaries of these body fragments and even their definitions become open to ceaseless negotiation. Here, Meursault's desire for Marie fails to map Marie's body; instead it, as Grosz articulates, "experiments, producing ever-new alignments, linkages, and connections, making things. It is fundamentally nomadic not teleological, meandering, creative, nonrepetitive, proliferative, unpredictable" (168).

When Meursault declares that he kisses Marie, he feigns to have total control over Marie and dissect her body into well-defined fragments. His kisses mainly censor, because they gloss over exchanges that menace Meursault's agency to map. The subversive potentialities of Marie's body, which Meursault seeks to persistently but unsuccessfully suppress, become manifest via a meticulous close reading between the lines: "On the dock, while we were drying ourselves off, [Marie] said, 'I'm darker than you.' I asked her if she wanted to go to the movies that evening" (20). Meursault immediately changes the topic when Marie claims that her body is darker. He refuses to reveal to the reader his reaction to Marie's words. Rather than a trivial observation that left no imprint on Meursault, Marie's remark could be loaded in a colonial setting wherein color represented a primary means of coding people.

Marie's body, just like the sun, can dethrone Meursault from his claim to eloquence, rationality and hegemony: "She lay down right next to me and the combined warmth from her body and from the sun made me doze off" (51). Marie's body, whose brown skin reflects a constant exposure to sun, attains a perfect symbiosis with nature and stands for the incandescent sun: "But the face I was looking for was as bright as the sun and the flame of desire—and it belonged to Marie" (119). The various connotations of this symbiosis provide a new perspective for Meursault's wish to kiss a man, since the ramifications of this wish tally with what many consider the novel's fulcrum—the murder of the Arab.

II

Camus's numerous essays on Algeria intermesh the imagery of kisses and the sun. The sun represents the very "center" of his generation's creative output that still seeks hope after the most calamitous segment of human history that witnessed two world wars, as he writes, "In the center of our work, dark though it may be, shines an inexhaustible sun, the same sun that shouts today across the hills and plain" ("The Enigma" 160–61).

Not surprisingly, many literary critics wrote about the sun motif in Camus's oeuvre.[1] Harold Bloom's observation below on the role of the sun in *The Stranger* is symptomatic of Camus scholarship:

> We have a vision of possession by the sun, an inferno that fuses consciousness and will into a single negation, and burns through it to purposes that may exist, but not are human. Gide's Lafcadio, a true absurdist, said he was not curious about events but about himself, while Meursault is

---

[1] For a more nuanced depiction of the sun in Camus's works, see Pourgouris 37–63. While he still projects the sun as a "reminder of the absurdity of the human condition" (48), Pourgouris nevertheless considers the sun an integral part of the Mediterranean eco-milieu in Camus's writings.

not curious about either. What Meursault at the end calls "the benign indifference of the universe" is belied by the pragmatic malevolence of the sun. The true influence upon *The Stranger* seems to me Melville's *Moby-Dick,* and for the whiteness of the whale Camus substitutes the whiteness of the sun. (*Albert Camus* 3–4)

This understanding of the sun abounds with Euro-American metaphysical concepts, such as consciousness, will, and negation. Many critics, like Bloom, transplant the sun, an element Camus considers an essential segment of the Algerian nature, into the midst of abstract philosophical debates that sever the sun's ties from its ecological surroundings. Camus complains during an interview in *Le Littéraire* that his critics, when embroiled in abstract Euro-American metaphysical concepts to interpret *The Stranger,* fail to discern "the importance of the Algerian atmosphere in *The Stranger*" ("Preface" 335).

To go against the grain of most critics who engaged in this "interpretive exploitation" of nature and reposition the sun back into its Algerian setting will help us discern that the sun and kisses represent two key signifiers counteracting the abstract reason that plagued Europe. For instance, Camus writes in "Nuptials in Tipasa," "We walk toward an encounter with love and desire. We are not seeking lessons or the bitter philosophy one requires of greatness. Everything seems futile here except the sun, our kisses, and the wild scents of the earth" (66).

Camus often expresses a wish for a mystical union between nature and his body, a consummative union captured through the imagery of kiss and embrace: "Yet even here, I know that I shall never come close enough to the world. I must be naked and dive into the sea, still scented with the perfumes of the earth, wash them off in the sea, and consummate with my flesh the embrace for which sun and sea, lips to lips, have so long been sighing" ("Nuptials in Tipasa" 68). Camus's artistic, emotional effusion stems from his deep, sensual communication with his own body and the nature. Camus draws a contrast in his essay "Summer in Algiers" between the people in Algiers who attain a perfect symbiosis with the sun and Europeans who feign naturalism under the pretentious vogue of nudism: "Not that [the young men in Algiers] have read the boring sermon of our nudists, those protestants of the body (there is a way of systematizing the body that is as exasperating as systems for the soul). They just 'like being in the sun'" (82). The sun provides a protective shield against the fossilized ways of systematizing the body; "at the center" of Camus's work lies an energy source that subverts corporeal systematizations that stand for "protestant" values.[2]

The estrangement from the body corresponds to the apotheosis of the soul: "The immortality of the soul, it is true, engrossed many noble minds. But this is because they reject the body, the only truth that is given them, before using up its strength" ("The Desert" 95). The following words in *The Stranger* demonstrate the court's incessant attempts to cement a soul for Meursault that tries to distance him from an embodied existence: "And I tried to listen again, because the prosecutor started talking about my soul" (100–01). The courtroom foments a narrative that symbolizes Meursault's moral deprivation through the image of his adulated soul, as the executioner declares, "I have never seen a soul as hardened as yours" (69).

While the French legal system creates Meursault's soul, it eradicates the Arab's body. Meursault's acts transcribed by other characters' minds as horrendous apathy—whether his nonchalant attitude in his mother's funeral or phlegmatic façade during the court case—accosts many people's sensibilities to such an extent that his sentencing to death seems more a punishment of this apathy than of the murder of the Arab. The French in the court need to ignore, as much as they can, the murder of the Arab and project it instead as a

---

[2] One perceives this aversion to abstract reason also in "The New Mediterranean Culture," a lecture by Camus in 1937 to mark the opening of a new community arts center in Algiers. It lays out the lineaments of Camus's particular vision of the Mediterranean. Camus depicts two cultures, Mediterranean and Latinate, the former celebrating corporeality, nature, cultural dialogue, and vigorous attachment to life, while the latter imposing nonpoetic abstract rationality that aggrandized the rift between East and West and exacerbated the burgeoning fascist movements of Europe. Camus's emphasis on the corporeality of one's experience also stems from his support for the Mediterranean culture. For a translation of this lecture and its contextualized study, see Foxlee.

matricide to transplant the murder from the subversive sun-drenched Algerian beach to the French-owned home for the elders. This transformation is captured in the prosecutor's words: "[A] man who is morally guilty of killing his mother severs himself from society in the same way as the man who raises a murderous hand against the father who begat him" (101–02).

We may discern the reason behind this erasure in the following sentence, just a few pages before the murder scene, that points to a silent stare peculiar to "them," the Arabs: "They were staring at us in silence, but in that way of theirs, as if we were nothing but stones or dead trees" (48). This stare reminds Meursault that he in the end is *nothing* but a stone or dead tree; the very foundations of his culture that deracinates its members from their bodies are nil and can easily crumble.

The harrowing anxiety that stems from this confrontation leads to the murder of the Arab. Meursault describes the murder scene: "The trigger gave; I felt the smooth underside of the butt; and there, in that noise, sharp and deafening at the same time, is where it all started. I shook off the sweat and sun" (59). Meursault attempts to break free from the shackles of the sun and sweat — elements that remind him of his corporeality — with the murder. In part I, the sun has a menacing presence for Meursault as a subject who maps the other.

The barrage of physical details that inundates the murder scene demonstrates this torturing effect of the sun that Meursault strongly wishes to escape from: "My eyes were blinded behind the curtain of tears and salt. All I could feel were the cymbals of sunlight crashing on my forehead and, indistinctly, the dazzling spear flying up from the knife in front of me" (59). He complains, "But today, with the sun bearing down, making the whole landscape shimmer with heat, it was inhuman and oppressive" (15). The sun, permeating through the ecological milieu, triggers a palpably harrowing oppression of an unlocalizable origin. Meursault suffers a painful disjuncture between himself and the space that encloses him.

Sara Ahmed writes in *Queer Phenomenology* that to be at home "is about becoming part of a space where one has expanded one's body, saturating the space with bodily matter" (11). Meursault can never enjoy this comfort, as his body becomes always hemmed in by the sun. The overpowering sun is not just in the sky; it instead shatters "into little pieces on the sand and water" (55). Its state becomes at times liquid and at times solid, blocking Meursault's movements: "And every time I felt a blast of its hot breath strike my face, I gritted my teeth, clenched my fists in my trouser pockets, and strained every nerve in order to overcome the sun and the thick drunkenness it was spilling over me. With every blade of light that flashed off the sand, from a bleached shell or a piece of broken glass, my jaws tightened" (57). Meursault feels suffocated and paralyzed within the whirlwind of Algerian sunlight.

The confrontation with the sun that queers boundaries drives Meursault to true dementia, inciting him to pull the trigger. Meursault approaches the cool spring behind the rock, where the murder would take place, to escape from the tortuous sun:

> From a distance I could see the small, dark mass of rock surrounded by a blinding halo of light and sea spray. I was thinking of the cool spring behind the rock. I wanted to hear the murmur of its water again, to escape the sun and the strain and the women's tears, and to find shade and rest again at last. But as I got closer, I saw that Raymond's man had come back.
> He was alone. He was lying on his back, with his hands behind his head, his forehead in the shade of the rock, the rest of his body in the sun. (57–58)

Meursault's adamant hankering for escaping from the sun becomes manifested especially in the source text, since he repeats the word *envie* (desire) three times in the same sentence when expressing his wish to avoid the sun; we never see Meursault so desirous again: "J'avais envie de retrouver le murmure de son eau, envie de fuir le soleil, l'effort et les pleurs de femme, envie de retrouver l'ombre et son repos" (*Œuvres* 1: 71). Here, Meursault momentarily relishes a frozen image of the Arab man in a cool spring, away from the sun, "his hands behind his head, his forehead in the shade of rock, the rest of his body in the sun." This description neatly fits into the narrative in which a colonizer maps scrupulously the body of the colonized.

Nevertheless, such a conceptualization soon gets undermined. Like all mirages that vanish with the slightest movement, his desire for a frozen image of the Arab proves insatiable; shortly thereafter, the Arab could draw his knife in the sun, whose light shot off the steel and "cut at [Meursault's] forehead" (59). Now under the sun, the Arab gains a menacing, anxiety-inducing presence: "Maybe it was the shadows on his face, but it looked like he was laughing" (58). In Meursault's murder, one discerns a counterreaction against the Algerian sun that dissects his body, which deprives Meursault of unity and autonomy that he desperately needs as a mapping subject: "The scorching blade slashed at my eyelashes and stabbed at my stinging eyes. *That's when everything began to reel*" (59, emphasis added). Here, the sun seems to adopt the role of the colonizer that maps and dissects the body of the colonized. It reminds Meursault that he can never have a noncorporeal and cerebral existence.

The Arab nurse represents another figure that disrupts the neat boundaries that postcolonial readings usually propagate. Both Edward Said and Timothy O'Brien rightly argue that discussions of existentialism, the absurd, or universal humanism ignore the murdered Arab and hence implicitly reinforce colonial, imperialist agendas.[3] Since the court trial shifts the focus from the murdered Arab to Meursault's mother, the machinations of the French legal system refuse to give adequate representation for the murdered Arab. For instance, O'Brien writes, "The relation of European to Arab, unlike the absolute impartiality of the Algiers court, is rooted in reality. It also works in the novel. The faceless Arabs, silently reappearing, help to make us feel the loneliness of the hero" (*Camus* 26). Yet not all Arabs are silent in *The Stranger*. The exclusive focus of Said's and O'Brien's readings on this lack of representation ironically silences another character that actually spoke in the novel—the Arab nurse, who appears briefly in the elder's house where Meursault's mother dies. Never once does O'Brien or Said write about her.

"The First Arab in *L'Etranger*" by Patrick McCarthy is the only work I could find on the Arab nurse. Understandably, McCarthy claims that the role of Arabs in Camus's writing needs more extensive studying, since most scholars focus exclusively on the murdered Arab. His article projects the Arab nurse as an element tamed to the colonial system: "Of all the Arab characters, she is the

---

[3] See Said 204–24.

only one who is seen to be working, and she reminds us that, while some of the others may be associated by Camus with the sun or the sea, none of them lives amidst nature. There is no pure nature in French Algeria and Arabs cannot escape the colonial system" (23). He describes the nurse as the embodiment of death: "Probing it Camus continues to associate the Arab nurse with death: her face is disfigured by a cancerous growth which will probably kill her" (24). Therefore, she has no political bearing: "But, rather than making her an object of political oppression like Raymond's mistress, her disease takes her outside of history" (24). Yet the nurse is far from a white face gnawed by cancer.[4] When we become attuned to multifarious connotations of the nurse's scarf, we confront a character who does not become subsumed into the colorless monotony of the elder's house.

Here is Meursault's first encounter with the Arab nurse: "Near the casket was an Arab nurse in a white smock, with a brightly colored scarf on her head" (6). We can easily discern the contrast between the elder's house, with its whitewashed walls, and its Arab nurse who wears a brightly colored headscarf. Here, the headscarf is the sole colored element that clutches Meursault's gaze.[5]

The nurse's presence is not disruptive just because she wears a colored headscarf. Imagine the immense magnitude of Meursault's discomfort when he observes that "[a]ll you could see of [the nurse's] face was the whiteness of the bandage" (7). Meursault cannot delineate the contours of the nurse's face, which looks like a blank page. This face remains outside the purview of Meursault's gaze that maps; therefore, the Algerian nurse instigates endless speculations in Meursault: "The nurse was on that side of the room too, but with her back to me. I couldn't see what she was doing. But the way her arms were moving made me think she was knitting" (9). The nurse's body

---

[4] McCarthy's claim here is not accurate; we never read in the novel that the nurse has a cancerous growth on her face, but instead only "an abscess" (7).

[5] The headscarf could also have disorientated Meursault because of its political connotations in the colonial milieu that could instantaneously trigger a wide palette of particular responses within anyone in Algeria. As a result, the veil sometimes stood for the most conspicuous signifier of resistance against colonial rule, as Frantz Fanon writes, "[F]or. . . the foreigner, the veil demarcates both Algerian society and its feminine component" (*A Dying Colonialism* 35–36).

does not conform to Meursault's wish to map and stabilize the other. It also reminds Meursault, as I shall soon argue, that he can never have a disembodied existence.

Unlike most previous literary critics who believed that Arabs represent decorative trinkets, playing no significant role in *The Stranger*, this unmappable Arab nurse plays a crucial role in shaping Meursault's mindset. For instance, only the Arab nurse breaks Meursault's indifference during Maman's funeral: "After that, everything seemed to happen so fast, so deliberately, so naturally that I don't remember any of it anymore. Except for one thing: as we entered the village, the nurse spoke to me" (17). In fact, despite her short yet momentous appearance, the words of the Arab nurse perhaps lead to the novel's key epiphany: "She said, 'If you go slowly, you risk getting sunstroke. But if you go too fast, you work up a sweat and then catch a chill inside the church.' She was right. There was no way out" (17). "There is no way out" of the sun, because Meursault's body can never remain shielded from it. This thought does not disappear from Meursault's mind, but instead doggedly haunts him, as he reflects in the prison:

> I moved closer to the window, and in the last light of day I gazed at my reflection one more time. It was still serious — and what was surprising about that, since at that moment I was too? But at the same time, and for the first time in months, I distinctly heard the sound of my own voice. I recognized it as the same one that had been ringing in my ears for many long days, and I realized that all that time I had been talking to myself. Then I remembered what the nurse at Maman's funeral said. No, there was no way out, and no one can imagine what nights in prison are like. (81)

The murder of the Arab on the beach did not delete the inextinguishable role of the Arab nurse in Meursault's psyche. Meursault moves "in the last light of day," and again realizes there is no way out — not necessarily out of the prison but out of the sun that never lets Meursault forget his embodied existence. This paragraph demonstrates that the French legal system failed to push Arabs into a fathomless silence. Instead, this system will always fail to remain insulated from the Arab voice and the sunlight. Even in the beginning of the trial, the courtroom cannot avoid the subversive characteristics of the sun: "The trial opened with the sun glaring outside" (82). The sun is an infiltrating agent that seeps through the courtroom blinds: "Despite the blinds, the sun filtered through in places and the air was already stifling" (83).

Neither does the decapitation represent the definitive end to these subversive characteristics. At first, decapitation could seem the authoritative finale that halts flux of energies characterizing the body in *The Stranger*. Meursault's "monstrosity" represents what cannot be contained in the French courtroom, which goads the prosecutor to plead for Meursault's execution: "For if in the course of what has been a long career I have had occasion to call for the death penalty, never as strongly as today have I felt this painful duty made easier, lighter, clearer by the certain knowledge of a sacred imperative and by the horror I feel when I look into a man's face and all I see is a monster" (102). The prosecutor discerns Meursault's monstrosity with peerless clarity, informed "by the certain knowledge of a sacred imperative."

It is perhaps no coincidence that the prosecutor declares this pellucid vision after Meursault admits that the sun was the main instigating factor behind the murder. What the prosecutor diagnoses as monstrosity could be Meursault's undeniably visible "queerness," as they confront a man, hitherto a French clerk, who now admits of his inability to escape from his embodiment in a sun-drenched environment. Patricia MacCormack acutely argues that body has been conceptualized as a monstrous pedestal that any subjectivity has to hinge upon in "The Queer Ethics of Monstrosity": "The body has traditionally been maligned as a monstrous necessity of human subjectivity. Bodies are the medium through which we access pleasure and horror beneath and beyond signifying and cleansing rituals that repress the knowledge that we all are vulnerable and volatile bodies" (257). The notions of monstrosity and queer, as MacCormack further observes, converge in their designation of uncontainable movement: "Monstrous bodies are also those that have certain qualities — sticky, not demarcated, compelling in spite of their repugnance, interspecies, multiple or generally resistant to both signification and subjectification" (257). To codify Meursault as a monster signifies the unmappability of his body.[6] Decapitation thus strives to cut an unsignifiable territory into clearly demarcated segments and thus exterminate this monstrosity.

Via decapitation, Meursault's head becomes the shared object of desire in the courtroom, as people await his execution to satiate it. Before the decapitation, we read that Meursault needs to have his "head cut off in a public square *in the name of the French people*" (107, emphasis added). The prosecutor also insists, "I ask you for [Meursault's] head" (102). Decapitation does not just signify the power's control over Meursault's body; it also attempts to stabilize and normativize the boundaries of corporeal localities. The head's boundaries become nonnegotiable through decapitation, which could halt the eddying queer movement prevalent in *The Stranger*. Indeed, Meursault often emphasizes the nonnegotiability that characterizes this decapitation: "It was an open-and-shut case, a fixed arrangement, a tacit agreement that there was no question of going back on" (111). Unlike this desire for decapitation, Meursault's wish to kiss a man opens up a novel avenue of experiencing desire that does not necessarily hinge upon a rigidly mapped body. This wish also reflects a much larger motif in the novel that abounds with elements challenging strict systematizations, such as the sun and Marie's body.

Among many questions that Meursault poses in the denouement of the novel, one particularly hints that even Meursault's decapitation cannot freeze the queer movements: "What did it matter that Marie now offered her lips to a new Meursault?" (121–22). This question, as many critics noted, clearly concretizes "the gentle indifference of the world" (122) that Meursault is discovering right before the execution. This queer reading suggests that this question also augurs a nonnormative future. Marie still will not "kiss" but

---

[6] Meursault's monstrosity could constitute a menace that should be obliterated also because life encounters its uttermost limitations not in the abyss of death but in the figure of the monster. Georges Canguilhem notes in "Monstrosity and the Monstrous", "It is monstrosity, not death, that is the countervalue to life. Death is the permanent and unconditional threat of the organism's decomposition; it is the limitation from outside, the negation of living by the nonliving. But monstrosity is the accidental and conditional threat of incompletion or distortion in the formation of form; it is the limitation from inside, the negation of the living by the nonviable" (188).

instead "offer" her lips even after Meursault's decapitation, instigating the exchange that undermines systematized corporeal cartographies. A new Meursault will survive through Marie's subversive kiss even after his execution that strived to fixate his corporeal boundaries. Hence, Meursault's decapitation cannot represent the authorial call in fossilizing corporeal mappings, nor can it normativize the definitions and boundaries of corporeal localities, just as the courtroom can never remain completely sheltered from the Arab voice or sunlight.

While Camus's creative output materializes his vision of the absurd that undermines pregiven normative values, it simultaneously delineates minute and yet pivotal moments, such as Meursault's articulation of a desire to kiss a man, that point to nebulous, "queer" corporeal cartographies that challenge pregiven mappings of the body. Such moments demonstrate that we do not glimpse the suburbs of the sensual only during the ephemeral instance when Meursault shares with the reader his desire to kiss a man for the first time in his life. *The Stranger* invites an incessant remapping of these suburbs, as it is not just people who articulate desires of same-sex affinity that inhabit them. One way of this remapping is to read closely, sensitively, and conscientiously the words of those hitherto deemed to enjoy heteronormativity. From these suburbs that constitute the rich literary landscape of Camus's oeuvre, we perceive even more clearly the murky grounds of heteronormativity that forcefully denies the queer, which always moves our lives in unexpected ways.

Author's note: Previous versions of this paper were presented at Harvard GSAS Gender & Sexuality Workshop and American Comparative Literature Association annual conference in 2013. I am grateful to organizers and participants for giving me the opportunity to share my work and for their useful feedback. I am also thankful to William Granara, Afsaneh Najmabadi, Suzanne Smith, and Karen Thornber for their continuous intellectual and emotional support.

Works cited

Ahmed, Sara. *Queer Phenomenology: Orientations, Objects, Others.* Durham: Duke University Press, 2006. Print.

Bloom, Harold. *Albert Camus.* New York: Chelsea House Publishers, 1989. Print.

Camus, Albert. "Nuptials at Tipasa." *Lyrical and Critical Essays.* Ed. Philip Thody. Trans. Ellen Conroy Kennedy. New York: Knopf, 1968. 65-72. Print.

---. *Œuvres Complètes.* Ed. Roger Grenier. Paris: Editions du Club de l'honnête homme, 1983. Print.

---. "Preface to *The Stranger.*" *Lyrical and Critical Essays.* Ed. Philip Thody. Trans. Ellen Conroy Kennedy. New York: Vintage Books, 1968. 335-37. Print.

---. "Summer in Algiers." *Lyrical and Critical Essays.* Ed. Philip Thody. Trans. Ellen Conroy Kennedy. New York: Knopf, 1968. 80-92. Print.

---. "The Desert." *Lyrical and Critical Essays.* Ed. Philip Thody. Trans. Ellen Conroy Kennedy. New York: Knopf, 1968. 93-105. Print.

---. "The Enigma." *Lyrical and Critical Essays.* Ed. Philip Thody. Trans. Ellen Conroy Kennedy. New York: Knopf, 1968. 154-61. Print.

---. *The Stranger.* Trans. Matthew Ward. New York: Vintage International, 1989. Print.

Canguilhem, Georges. "Monstrosity and Monstrous." Trans. Chris Turner. *The Body: A Reader.* Ed. Mariam Fraser and Monica Greco. New York: Routledge, 2005. 187–93. Print.

Carroll, David. *Albert Camus, the Algerian: Colonialism, Terrorism, Justice.* New York: Columbia University Press, 2007. Print.

Fanon, Frantz. *A Dying Colonialism.* Trans. Haakon Chevalier. New York: Grove Press, 1967. Print.

Foxlee, Neil. *Albert Camus's "the New Mediterranean Culture": A Text and its Contexts.* Oxford: Peter Lang, 2010. Print.

Grosz, Elizabeth. *Volatile Bodies: Toward a Corporeal Feminism.* Bloomington: Indiana University Press, 1994. Print.

MacCormack, Patricia. "The Queer Ethics of Monstrosity." *Speaking of Monsters: A Teratological Anthology.* Ed. Caroline Joan S. Picart and John Edgar Browning. New York: Palgrave Macmillan, 2012. 255-67. Print.

McCarthy, Patrick. "The First Arab in L'Etranger." *CELFAN Review* IV.3 (1985): 23-26. Print.

O'Brien, Conor Cruise. *Camus*. London: Fontana, 1970. Print.

Pourgouris, Marinos. *Mediterranean Modernisms: The Poetic Metaphysics of Odysseus Elytis*. Burlington, VT: Ashgate, 2011. Print.

Said, Edward W. *Culture and Imperialism*. New York: Knopf, 1994. Print.

Sedgwick, Eve Kosofsky. *Tendencies*. Durham: Duke University Press, 1993. Print.

ALBERT CAMUS AS RHETORICAL PLAYWRIGHT: THE EMBODIMENT OF HIS ETHIC IN DRAMA

by Jeffry C. Davis

> In a universe suddenly divested of illusions and lights,
> man feels an alien, a stranger. His exile is without
> remedy since he is deprived of the memory of a lost
> home or the hope of a promised land. This divorce
> between man and his life, the actor and his setting, is
> properly the feeling of absurdity.
>
> — ALBERT CAMUS, *The Myth of Sisyphus*

Many scholars recognize that Albert Camus never considered himself to be an existentialist, nor did he prefer to be labeled as a philosopher. As Germaine Bree explains, Camus avoided the endeavor to construct a systematic philosophical presentation of the human condition in the world: "In fact, he had a rational aversion toward all such systems. Perhaps because of his background he was much more interested in becoming, in a Socratic sense, a man with an ethic" (Albert Camus 10). Camus did not oppose the title of "writer," however, for through his writing he struggled to explore his ethic for living with intelligibility. As Stephen Eric Bronner asserts, "Camus was always concerned with the craft of writing, and the form is inextricably interwoven with the content. His writing crosses the boundaries between art, politics, and philosophy. It constitutes a single exercise in symbolic action" (163). Popularly known as the author of several novels and essays, including *The Stranger, The Myth of Sisyphus, The Plague, The Rebel,* and *The Fall,* Camus was recognized for his talent as a writer in 1957, when he received the Nobel Prize in Literature "for his important literary production, which with clear-sighted earnestness illuminates the problems of the human conscience in our times" ("Albert Camus—Facts"). In his acceptance speech, Camus clarified, "The writer's role is not free from difficult duties. By definition he cannot put himself today in the service of those who make history; he is at the service of those who suffer it" ("Albert Camus—Banquet Speech").

Not as commonly known is the fact that drama, of all the various literary genres, represented the expressive form that Camus valued with the highest regard. As E. Freeman elucidates in The Theater of Albert Camus, "Above all, and more than for social and psychological reasons, Camus devoted himself to the theater throughout his life because he believed it to be the greatest form of artistic expression" (3). From his early years as a passionate new member of the Communist Party in Algiers, where he founded Le Theatre du Travail 'Worker's Theater' in 1935, to the exciting years from 1944 to 1949 when his four plays were all performed professionally in Paris by some of the best talents in French theater, until his tragic death in 1960, at which time he had been appointed to be the director of a state-subsidized experimental theater — Albert Camus exhibited constant devotion to the theater during his lifetime, giving testimony to his great dedication to the dramatic form. As a playwright, Camus embodied his beliefs about the absurd, and his ethic for living, through his four original theatrical creations — *Caligula, Cross Purpose, State of Siege,* and *The Just* — which have been generally overlooked as a corpus, relative to his better known novels and essays.

Before considering Camus' plays, an examination of his ethic for living in the face of the absurd is warranted. No work describes his ethic better than The Myth of Sisyphus. Reflecting upon the Greek mythological character Sisyphus — who suffers the fate of having to push a bolder up a mountain, only to watch it roll back down again, and then chase after it, repeating the process endlessly — Camus examines a fundamental human question: *Is life really worth living?*

"The meaning of life," Camus begins, "is the most urgent of questions" (*Myth* 4). Curiously, he sets forth by describing the frequently mundane quality of human existence. Human beings find themselves constrained to daily habits that numb them from the truth about themselves and the world: rising... eating... working... eating... working... eating... sleeping—day after day, week after week, month after month, year after year. "But one day the 'why' arises and everything begins in that weariness tinged with amazement," and, as Camus observes, in an unexpected moment "the impulse of consciousness" prevails for some, bringing the realization of the monotony and illusion of the human situation (*Myth* 13). This heightened mindfulness leads to the dramatic recognition that genuine meaning cannot be attained from an inscrutable world:

> The primitive hostility of the world rises up to face us across millennia. For a second we cease to understand it because for centuries we have understood in it solely the images and designs that we had attributed to it beforehand, because henceforth we lack the power to make use of that artifice. The world evades us because it becomes itself again. That stage scenery masked by habit becomes again what it is. It withdraws at a distance from us.... that denseness and that strangeness of the world is the absurd. (*Myth* 14)

Theater discourse and drama metaphors augment the persuasive message of passages such as this; in fact, Marie-Louise Audin astutely detects the use of theatrical vocabulary throughout the essay (105). As Camus implies through his use of this language, for those who can rightly apprehend the "artifice" of life there is a stark revelation: the longstanding significations of meaning, "the images and designs," simply do not work, and the scripted scenes and acting behaviors, the "stage scenery masked by habit," cannot be sustained. Suddenly the world is no longer what it has for so long appeared to be. Therefore, once the theatrical props of day-to-day living become exposed, a terrible sense of alienation from the familiar results. Those solitary creatures who rightly perceive the stage apparatus of life nevertheless still feel compelled to seek out meaning, despite the apparent impossibility of the undertaking. Yet, reason, the only tool to take on the task, proves to be too limited to adequately extract an answer from a world that is now unavoidably filled with complex incongruities, involving desire, power, and violence. Amihud Gilead aptly interprets the situation Camus portrays: "Our reason cannot explain and understand everything" (336). By their nature, human beings need meaning to exist; nevertheless, by its very nature, the world resists the artifice of coherent answers, leading to the condition Camus describes as *absurdity*. "The absurd," explains Camus, "is born of this confrontation between the human need and the unreasonable silence of the world" (Myth 28). Absurdity, then, is not simply defined as the external state of chaos and opacity in the world, or merely the internal dilemma resulting when humans face reality as it is; rather, it arises out of the engagement of the two: "The Absurd is not in man...nor in the world, but in their presence together" (Camus, *Myth* 30). Consequently, the absurd poses an intractable, truly dramatic dilemma, which Camus presents with rhetorical force, a dilemma that elicits a deliberate reaction.

For those who see the world through the lens of the absurd, several responses become apparent, including nihilism, despair, suicide or even metaphysical hope; yet, none of these responses, according to Camus, provides a legitimate solution. Robert Zaretsky points out, "Camus insisted that absurdity does not lead to a nihilistic life. On the contrary, the very ability to acknowledge the absurd requires a moral effort" (6). Similarly, to assert that the world is meaningless represents a totalizing conclusion, a certainty not afforded by the absurd. Thus, how to live well in the absence of certainty becomes the ethical question. Flirting with the possibility of becoming a nihilist as a young man, and eventually realizing this pursuit's dehumanizing effects, "Camus felt that the nihilism responsible for having brought the Nazis into power was now threatening the entire world" (Rhein 67). Correspondingly, Camus believed the move to embrace despair turns human potential toward a destructive end. Despair proves to be a weak moral choice for a bleak existence; it lacks defiant energy, and therefore it remains untenable. Karen D. Hoffman asserts that "For Camus, the proper response to despair must be a human one, generated by human solidarity, love, and common decency" (337). Clearly, Camus' ethic for living demands more that mere individual consideration. This is one reason why suicide, an irreversible response to despair, though decisive, does not actively sustain a confrontation with the absurd and cannot be endorsed. Killing one's self only gives in to despair — "suicide settles the absurd" (Camus, *Myth* 54) — functioning as the illogical response to the realization that life does not afford ultimate, unequivocal understanding. Likewise, the decision to conjure up hope in some transcendent eschaton is an escape from the actual scheme of things, a type of intellectual suicide. Taking the "leap of faith," as Kierkegaard did, violates the premise of facing life according to what one can know about it for certain. In this light, Hank S. Weddington considers Camus' view of religious hope as a choice to embrace illusion: "He contended that the religious attitude is a grasp at transcendental hope and surrender to nostalgia. Nostalgia becomes an escape or avoidance of the absurd for it clings to a notion that reason will prevail or that an ideal state will be achieved" (123). For Camus, metaphysical hope emanates from what cannot be singularly known through reason, as he voices with disquiet: "It is not the affirmation of God that is questioned here, but rather the logic leading to that affirmation" (*Myth* 42). If logic alone were sufficient for belief in God, then all rational people would believe, and metaphysical explanations of the world would meet the abiding needs of human beings. Maria K. Genovese emphasizes, "In an absurd world, God is no longer available to provide order or comfort" (3). Such succor demands something beyond reason. Nihilism, despair, suicide, and hope — all represent false choices for Camus, poor responses for those compelled to acknowledge the power of the absurd; they deny the resilience of humanity, to exist as rational beings, and subsequently these options cannot provide ultimately satisfying answers in response to absurdity.

The only option left for a human being in the face of the absurd is to live life to its fullest, despite the world's refusal in providing rational, ultimate solutions. This option Camus terms as "revolt," a bold defiance against the absurd, his *raison d'être*: "the constant confrontation between man and his own obscurity" (Myth 54). Revolt requires lucidity, the sustained ability to see oneself and the world honestly. Only with this kind of authenticity can one engage the truth of mortality, realizing the evident and inescapable temporality of human existence, which paradoxically can be liberating. "The absurd enlightens me on this point: there is no future. Henceforth this is the reason for my inner freedom" (Camus, *Myth* 58). David Carroll notes this kind of "absurd reasoning," that recognizes the lack of remedy for the world's meaninglessness, becomes the very basis for resisting despair and embracing life (55-56). Revolt is the only viable option for Camus because it allows the honest exercise of reason — "To an absurd mind reason is useless and there is nothing beyond reason" (Myth 58) — while concomitantly it provides freedom and a sense of resolute inviability — "He enjoys a freedom with regard to common rules" (Myth 59). Human beings must persevere in spite of their absurd existence, like Sisyphus. Yet, Camus believes that the best human response involves becoming autonomous — a master of one's own fate — just as Sisyphus was, by the mere fact that he chose to go back down the mountain after the rock and begin all over again. Camus exalts, "I leave Sisyphus at the foot of the mountain! One always finds one's burden again... but Sisyphus teaches the higher fidelity that negates the gods and raises the rocks. He concludes that all is well... the struggle itself toward the heights is enough to fill a man's heart. One must imagine Sisyphus happy" (Myth 123).

Camus' theory of art naturally stems from his ethic for living. The function of art, Camus stresses, ought to be understood relative to Friedrich Nietzsche: "'Art is nothing but art,' said Nietzsche, 'we have art in order not to die of the truth'" (Myth 93). Yet, this quotation should not be misunderstood to suggest that art prevents humans from engaging the truth: such a view would be in direct opposition to Camus' belief in the necessity of lucidity. Instead, Camus recognizes, with Nietzsche, that art has the power to convey the truth of life, especially the absurd condition of existence, and in so doing art can become a source of lucidity. Essential for authentic survival, art-based lucidity prevents human beings from remaining blind to their problematic situation, and it keeps them from falling back into numbing routines. "So it is with the work of art," maintains Camus. "If the commandments of the absurd are not respected, if the work does not illustrate divorce and revolt, if it sacrifices to illusions and arouses hope, it ceases to be gratuitous" (Myth 102). Thus, art must not reinforce delusion or provide escapism, nor should it offer a popular audience saccharine grounds for contentment. As Camus argues in Resistance, Rebellion and Death, "If it adapts itself to what the majority of our society wants, art will be a meaningless recreation" (253). The artist, then, must not deny the truth of reality. On the contrary, Camus insists that it is the artist's responsibility to exist in ambiguity—"incapable of negating the real and yet eternally unfinished aspects" (Resistance 264). The role of the artist, then, is to create work that is serious, providing lucidity through the medium used, and accordingly promoting liberty. Real art promotes the audience's ability to engage mortality and to live radically. "Camus therefore rejects a purely abstract conception of the work of art. Art, if it is to be honest to reality...must also interrogate the forms in which humans come together in resistance against the absurd" (Simpson 387). Such interrogation of the forms for resistance demands that art, in a real sense, persuades the audience to revolt against the absurd.

No form, no artistic medium, was better able to embody Camus' theory of art than the play written for production. Why? On the stage women and men—living flesh and blood—can act. They can speak, wonder, doubt, fear and, most of all, move an audience in a span of fleeting time amazingly analogous to the measure of one's own lifetime. Still more, characters can raise crucial questions about the very nature of one's life. As Lévi-Valensi writes, "Le théâtre est, pour Camus, un engagement de tout l'être." 'Theater is, for Camus, an engagement of one's entire being.' (15). Like Shakespeare's Hamlet, Camus saw the play as the thing wherein to "catch the conscience" (Shakespeare 2.2, line # 606), especially of the audience, jolting it toward a poignant glimpse of reality. "The actor has three hours to be Iago or Alceste, Phaedre or Gloucester," declares Camus. "In that short space of time he makes them come to life and die on fifty square yards of boards. Never has the absurd been so well illustrated or at such length" (Myth 78). The Stage therefore essentially accomplished two closely related things for Camus: first, it was a vehicle by which the Platonic assertion "The unexamined life is not worth living" (Apology 38a) could be embodied through characters, thereby confronting his audience with lucidity; and second, it was also the means by which he fulfilled his own revolt in the face of the absurd, thereby presenting elements of his own ethic for living, compellingly rendered through drama.

It is important to note that Camus, in common with such dramatists as Jean-Paul Sartre, Simone de Beauvior and Gabriel Marcel, "used the theater primarily as a medium for expression and dramatization of serious ideas" during a time when France was experiencing great turbulence (Cruickshank, Introduction 20). The years just prior to World War II were—politically, socially, ideologically, and artistically—frenzied with nervous energy. There was a need to rethink the violent planet in light of human agency, especially given the brutal memories of World War I, with the impending fears of World War II on the horizon. Within this tension-filled milieu, Camus offered his ethic for living, largely through the French theater, attempting, like his contemporaries, to deal with the topsy-turvy order of things. This great sense of urgency among the dramatists of pre-World War II France to redefine meaning in life characterized the beginning of an era of superb artistic creativity in the theater. "In the decade before the First World War the French theater was at its lowest ebb. Twenty-five years later, on the eve of the Second World War, it was in the process of becoming better than it had ever been since the seventeenth century...unsurpassed in theatrical brilliance and philosophical insight" (Freeman 1).

Aware that the French theater was experiencing rejuvenation in the 1930s, and hence giving new direction to society, Camus gave serious consideration to the distinctive means by which he would achieve his purposes upon the stage with profound effect, including the following. First, influenced by the Greeks and Nietzsche, Camus saw tragedy as the most appropriate form of drama for the twentieth century. With its Apollo-Dionysus opposition, the tragic form, as Bree states, "is born out of the conflict between two equally strong, equally valid antagonistic forces, man's passionate assertion of his freedom and will to live, and the irreducible natural order to which he must submit" (Camus 147). Additionally, Robert Wade Kenny links the poetics of tragedy with the rhetorics of tragedy, affirming a strong interchange between tragic drama and speech; furthermore, he recognizes Camus, and his Sisyphus, as an exemplar: "The task of the rhetor of tragedy is to plausibly craft such narrative in keeping with the sheltering and unsheltering of the *ethos* of the *polis*. Tragedy, in this sense, is a discourse that plays a fundamental role in humanity's ongoing destiny as a rising and a falling, constituting and reconstituting the world" (121). All four of Camus' original tragedies exhibit such vicissitudes Second, unlike almost every other great French dramatist of the 1930s, including Anouilh and Cocteau, who went to the Greeks at least once for a myth relating to the dilemma of the modern age, Camus leaned away from such a trend. Camus offers a variety of other more modern narratives, mostly European: from the story of the Roman emperor Caligula, going on a destructive rampage (which, though ancient, is rendered with strikingly contemporary characterization and dialog); to the efforts of the ordinary townspeople of Cadiz, attempting to throw off tyranny; to the struggle of terrorists during the Russian Revolution, plotting to kill the Grand Duke; to a bizarre family reunion gone wrong in Bohemia, resulting in multiple deaths. Camus placed his plays in diverse narrative contexts with strikingly evocative effects. Third, to enhance this up-to-date tragic form, Camus worked carefully to craft an innovative style of dialog: a mixture between classical and modern French, giving the audience a feel of fragmented familiarity, thus enhancing the sense of the absurd. Yet, Camus did not believe in using language to overtly jar or disturb in order to convey a sense of the absurd. Fourth, and related, in keeping with his emphasis upon reasoning and of a "theater of ideas," Camus avoided manipulation: "I have little regard for an art that deliberately aims to shock because it is unable to convince" (Preface vi). Because of these artistic aspects, Camus' drama possesses stylistic force, locating the audience members within an exchange of artistic persuasion. Camus' theater, as Sartre would agree, is a theater of situation rather than deep psychological penetration. The characters are portrayed not for their intrinsic value but to embody ideas and to act within moral constraints, portraying more the human condition rather than any particular human being's condition. Engaging the intellect, more than the emotions, Camus stylistically seeks to convey his ethic for living through his drama, all in an attempt to change people's minds more than their hearts. Therefore, his dramatic art can be viewed as theatrical rhetoric; and his foremost role as an artist can be considered to be as a rhetorical playwright, writing in service to his ethic.

With Camus' ethic for living now examined, though certainly not exhaustively so, and his rhetorical approach as a playwright contextualized within the "theater of ideas," an exploration of the specific ideas that constitute his ethic, as they are manifest in his plays, can now ensue with greater perspicuity.

Camus' first play, Caligula, was written in 1938. More than any of his other plays, Caligula displays the various stages a human being may go through in the process toward revolt: a revolt, in this case, that is invalid to Camus. Based on Suetonius' Lives of the Twelve Caesars, the plot unfolds in the first act with young Prince Caligula agonizing over the sudden death of his sister—and mistress—Drusilla. This encounter with mortality shakes Caligula's comfortable regal life, and as a result he alienates himself, running out into the wilderness to think, far away from his faithful friend Helicon, his second mistress Caesonia, his patricians, and the rest of the citizens of his kingdom. When Caligula finally returns to his palace, three days later, he is all covered with mud, damp from the rain. While peering into a full-length mirror at his disheveled body, Helicon walks on stage and kindly asks where he has been. Caligula responds by saying that he has been searching for the moon. "I'm not mad," says the prince, "in fact I've never felt so lucid... Really this world of ours, the scheme of things as they call it, is quite intolerable. That's why I want the moon or happiness, or eternal life—something, in fact, that may sound crazy, but which isn't of this world" (Camus, Caligula 39-40). Caligula goes on to tell Helicon that while he has been away he has discovered a truth: "Men die; and they are not happy" (Camus, Caligula 40). This statement serves as a clear sign that lucidity has crashed in upon Caligula, requiring him to battle with his own sense of absurdity.

After an initial period of despair in Act I, Caligula strives to rebel against the absurd situation in which he finds himself by attempting to make the impossible possible during Acts II and III. The moon, a symbol of the unattainable, is Caligula's obsession, and he makes Helicon promise to do his best to obtain it. "All I want, Helicon, is—the moon. For the rest, I've always known what will kill me" (Camus, Caligula 77). Having already come to terms with his own mortality, vicariously through the death of Drusilla, Caligula finds himself free from constraints. Intrepidly daring to exercise his liberties to their extreme, and justified by a sense of perverse logic, Caligula causes chaos in his kingdom through the following despicable acts:

indescriminately executing citizens; overtly engaging in sexual relations with the wife of one of his patricians; brazenly opening "Caligula's National Brothel" and awarding "the Badge of Civic Merit" to the citizen who patronizes there the most; and sadistically declaring a national famine for his subjects. He becomes, for Camus, as Phillip Thody suggests, "what Undershaft was for Shaw — a figure who is horribly right because things as they are are horribly wrong" (16). As Caligula states himself, "One is always free at someone else's expense. Absurd perhaps, but so it is" (Camus, *Caligula* 60). Caligula takes nihilism to its extreme in his inferior attempt at revolting against the absurd. His selfish indulgences only serve to worsen the world around him, making it more absurd for his people than it was for him when he first considered the ontological meaning of Drusilla's death. Rather than revolting constructively, Caligula ironically promotes the very evil he despises, perpetuating misery, for which he must eventually pay dearly.

In the final act, Caligula looks in the mirror as he did just prior to the beginning of his tirade in the first act. Then pondering what he should do, he reflects on what he has already done. "My time is short...I shant have the moon. Never, never, never!...I have chosen a wrong path, a path that leads to nothing. My freedom isn't the right one" (Camus, *Caligula* 103). Paul Corey sees the ending of this play as a logical assent to mortality, especially given that Caligula has become indifferent to everything — including his own life (68). The exercise of freedom without a sense of human dignity and sanctity of life, as Camus makes evident, is nothing better than cruel despotism. In this regard, John Cruickshank perceives striking similarities between Caligula and Hitler — their oppressive megalomania, their twisted mindsets, their perverse behaviors, and their self-induced deaths (Albert Camus 198-99). Two ironic conclusions emerge through Caligula's violent demise. First, revolt without a clear moral code can never be acceptable. Second, chaos and suffering perpetuated by people like Caligula will persist, as symbolically suggested by Caligula's last words, "I'm still alive!" (Camus, *Caligula* 104).

Whereas Caligula explores the implications of one man's actions in response to the absurd, *Cross Purpose* (also translated as The Misunderstanding) considers more intensely the nature of the human condition: "one of sterility, exile and death in a world governed by the absurd" (Freeman 60). The play received criticism by many as being oppressive, a charge Camus never denied. He wrote it during the Nazis occupation, when he was a member of the French Resistance hiding high in the mountains of Central France. Alone, confined, cut off from his wife, friends, and relatives, Camus conveys his own sense of isolation into the play, reflecting the situation in which he wrote it in 1943. "It is true that its atmosphere is suffocating," Camus acknowledged. "But we were all out of breath at that time" (Preface vii). The setting of the play, a small, quiet inn in a remote, dreary, rainy, little town in Czechoslovakia, provides a natural environment in which lack of communication, blind action, and pain can occur. While Caligula is a tragedy of a man decisively acting in the wrong ways, Cross Purpose is a tragedy of characters unable to fully act, overwhelmed by the cruelty of existence.

The plot, similar to the story found on a piece of newspaper under Meursault's mattress in The Stranger, is a tragic variation of the parable of the prodigal son. After twenty years away from his family, the son comes back home to his family's inn, now a wealthy man, only to be unrecognized by his sister and mother and then murdered by them in the night for monetary gain. Jan, the son, is compelled to leave his country of "endless sunshine beside the sea" (Camus, *Cross Purpose* 114) and find a sense of belonging again. His wife, Maria, who comes to the town with Jan, is put up in another hotel so that Jan can experience the anticipated reunion unencumbered by the need to immediately explain his wife. As Jan tells Maria before he leaves her, "One cannot remain a stranger all one's life. It is quite true man needs happiness, but he also needs to find his true place in the world. And I believe that coming back to my country, making the happiness of those I love, will help me to do this" (Camus, *Cross Purpose* 117). Indeed, ironically Jan is received by his mother and sister as the anticipated source of "happiness," for as they believe, after years of systematically murdering wealthy guests, only one more murder is needed to provide them with enough money to leave their miserable life at the inn behind. The mother continually says that she feels tired and that she needs a long rest. She represents a person worn down by the routines of hard work, vaguely aware of her need for change—for revolt. The daughter,

Martha, is bitter over her cloistered life, letting her anger motivate her determination to murder Jan, with the help of her mother. "Once we have enough money in hand," Martha excitedly tells her mother, "and I can escape from this inn and this dreary town where it's always raining; once we've forgotten this land of shadows — ah then, when my dream has come true, and we're living beside the sea, then you will see me smile" (Camus, *Cross Purpose* 109). Happiness is the ultimate end for Martha and her mother, as well as for Jan. Their desire for contentment rises out of their dissatisfaction with their individual lives, their experience of the world, and their lack of a meaningful purpose.

In the last act, Camus shows the characters to be what they truly are: victims of their own desperately absurd circumstances who are unable to act with an ethic. When Maria comes to the inn to find her husband, the morning after he has been drugged and thrown into the river, the truth becomes apparent to all. The play then concludes tragically: the mother drowns herself; Martha hangs herself; and Maria begs God for help through a prayer, to which, when she finishes, the old deaf manservant responds with a sardonic "No," ending the play. Jan's reluctance to tell his mother and sister who he actually is, his inability to be honest, prevents lucidity for everyone, and precludes authentic revolt for all. However, the play's message does not seem to say, "If only Jan had given his true identity, they all would have lived happily ever after." This would be too optimistic for Camus. The play does not expose people who wear masks in order to show the need for these people to remove them, a common theme in Pirandello's plays. Cross Purpose, like the title itself hints, depicts what one is to expect from life on this earth: unintentional conflict from a lack of comprehension. With this being the case, there is little natural cause for happiness. Just as it is impossible for Vladimir and Estragon to escape their situation in Waiting for Godot, it is doubtful that Jan, even if he had been clear about his identity, could have made his dreams, or the dreams of his mother and sister, come true. Camus does not see the pursuit of happiness as a plausible option in a world where the abnormal pervades as normal. The best that one can do, as this play reveals, is to strive to live with lucidity and continued revolt (not suicide or faith in God); this becomes especially poignant since, as Heinz Moenkemeyer reminds, "misunderstanding, which furnishes the title of the play, is a basic feature of human existence" (62).

In State of Siege, written in 1948, Camus experiments stylistically to achieve a novel dramatic effect. Theatrically, he mingles "all the different forms of dramatic expression, from a lyrical monologue to a collective theatre, through dumb show, straightforward dialogue, farce, and the use of chorus" (Thody 40). Probably because of these innovations, in part, the play was received very poorly in Paris. Furthermore, critics expected the work to be a dramatization of Camus' novel *The Plague*, which was published the year before, and although the subject matter is similar, the rendering is quite different. As Camus himself said, "Truly, few plays have ever enjoyed such a unanimous slashing" (Preface vii).

State of Siege begins with an omen comet in the sky, and the coming of The Plague, a symbolic character representing the absurd who arrives in the city of Cadiz, overthrows the established government and starts a random extermination of the inhabitants. The people of Cadiz, stricken with fear, wonder what they have done to bring on such a catastrophe. Their sin, as conveyed through the Governor's speech prior to The Plague's coming, is that they have become enraptured with their own comfortable existence. "Worthy townsfolk, your Governor wishes you a good day. He is pleased to see you gathered here as usual and carrying on with the activities that ensure the peace and prosperity of Cadiz. I am glad to see that nothing's changed, for that is as it should be. I like my habits, and change is the one thing I detest" (Camus, *State of Siege* 150). The people of Cadiz, bureaucratically manipulated by their self-seeking city officials, have become victims of their own malaise, and prime candidates for encountering the truth of their mortality through The Plague. It is because the government functions in such an anesthetized way that it is unable to resist The Plague's invasion and subsequent havoc. Here Camus verges on the mode of allegory, as E. Freeman clarifies: "The dictatorship [of The Plague] is a synthesis of Stalinism, Nazism and Italian and Spanish Fascism" (77). In this play Camus rebukes fascism and, even more, the ineffective governments that allow it to develop. It is because people and governments become numb and unaware of injustice that fascism of Franco's brand comes into being. As Camus recognizes, in the presence of fascism, liberty — of any kind — simply cannot exist.

Rising out of the mass of terrified citizens, Diego, the young hero of the play, after considering his own mortality, becomes free from his fear of death and challenges The Plague. Inciting rebellion, Diego shouts to his fellow men, "Stand up I tell you and act like men! Tear up your certificates, smash the windows of their offices, and shout your freedom to the four winds of heaven!" (Camus, *State of Siege* 211). It is because Diego looses his fear of death, and shows the town's people that they can loosen their fear, too, that Cadiz becomes immune to the evil power that The Plague initially holds upon them. The Plague, only able to control those who fear him, realizes he has lost the battle. Yet, in his last attempt to gain control, he strikes a bargain with Diego. Having already infected Diego's fiancé, Victoria, with the disease, The Plague offers her to Diego in exchange for the city. Diego refuses the offer, instead substituting his own life as a sacrifice for the city and Victoria. Jason Herbeck perceptively observes that Diego represents the first Camusian protagonist who accepts full responsibility for choosing, with a conscious awareness of the consequences — life or death (129). Camus shows, by the end of the play, that revolts must take the value of human lives into account; such lives — insignificant as they may seem to oppressors — possess incalculable significance.

Similarly, the preciousness of human life and the limitations of revolt serve as the central themes examined in Camus' last play, The Just (also translated as The Just Assassins), written in 1949. Set in pre-revolutionary Russia in the year 1905, the play begins with great tension in the apartment of the revolutionaries, where they wait to hear important news: has their comrade Kaliayev accomplished his mission and thrown a bomb into the passing carriage of the corrupt Grand Duke. When Kaliayev arrives, all distraught and shaken, his friends learn that he could not bring himself to throw the bomb for a good reason: the Duke's young niece and nephew rode in the carriage with him. Despite taunting accusations of a lack of commitment to the revolutionary cause by the young radical Stephen, Kaliayev insists that he did the right thing. "I was going to have to throw it at them . . . just like that . . . straight at them . . . Oh, no! . . . I just couldn't do it!" (Camus, *The Just* 183). The conflict of ideologies between Stephen, who has already been hardened after suffering through a prison sentence at the order of the Duke, and Kaliayev, who is still sensitive and committed to the worth of human life, demonstrates two paths that Camus sees with regard to violent revolt. For Stephen, the acquisition of personal liberties that will eventually the spread across the land is easily worth the execution of two innocent children. Yet, such disregard for a just kind of violence is detestable to Dora, Kaliayev's devoted lover, who sees the day coming when violent men like Stephen will dominate the world, lacking the scruples of a just assassin like Kaliayev. When Dora speaks her mind to Stephen, "Even destruction has a right and a wrong way, and there are limits," he quickly cuts her off: "There are no limits. What it really means is that you don't believe in the revolution!" (Camus, *The Just* 187).

Clearly, Camus sides with Kaliayev, who differentiates between constructively revolting against a corrupt government—a concrete manifestation of the absurd—and simply adding to, and becoming a part of, the collective ataxia of the human race. The differentiating factor for Kaliayev is his ethic for living, a moral directive based on his high regard for individual life. The ethic not only informs him of his limits (e.g. not killing small children), it also makes him aware that he must be willing to sacrifice his own life as just retribution for any life he takes. When Kaliayev eventually makes another attempt upon the Duke's life, and succeeds, he knows he has done it in the spirit of his ethic for living—and dying. After he is caught, the Grand Duchess visits him in jail before his execution and asks him to speak about his crime. "What crime?," he responds, "I remember only an act of justice . . . He [the Duke] was the living, human symbol of the supreme injustice which the Russian people have suffered for centuries! In return for that . . . he received only privileges! But I . . . even if I am wrong . . . my wages are prison and death" (Camus, *The Just* 212). Kaliayev accepts his execution with dignity and perishes, though only a peasant, more nobly than the Duke; he dies according to his ethic. As Maurice Weyembergh concludes regarding the protagonists of this play, they demonstrate a viable political option, a glimmer of light in the midst of darkness (181).

Beginning with Caligula and ending with Kaliayev, Camus comes full circle in exploring his ethic for living as an authentic human being and, in particular, the options for action—particularly of revolt—available to the person who courageously faces the absurd. Remarkably, as Martin Esslin explains in The Theatre of the Absurd, though Camus is largely responsible for defining "the absurd," his drama does not belong to the genre of the Theatre of the Absurd. "The Theatre of the Absurd," explains Esslin, "strives to express its sense of the senselessness of the human condition and the inadequacies of the rational devices and discursive thought. While Sartre or Camus express the new content in the old convention, the Theatre of the Absurd goes a step further in trying to achieve a unity between its basic assumptions and the form in which these are expressed" (6). Clearly, Camus' "old convention" represents his insistence upon recognizing human reason as essential to personal experience; flawed as it is, reason helps to make as much sense out of this nonsensical and violent existential situation as possible, and it illuminates options for deliberate living. As has been discussed, Camus accomplishes this through words and ideas, rhetorically exhibited, more than action upon the stage. This emphasis upon words goes against Antonin Artaud's theory that "words do not mean everything, and that by their nature and defining character, fixed once and for all, they arrest and paralyze thought instead of permitting it and fostering its development" (Esslin 335). Artaud's aesthetic statement corresponds with Eric Bentley's major criticism of Camus' drama, although Bentley sees a slightly different result of Camus using words, over and above actions. "There are too many key speeches,'" says Bentley, "speeches after which one can say 'Oho, so that's what the play's about,' speeches that would not be necessary if the drama had been concentrated in the action and the characters" (In Search of Theater 47). As he goes on to explain in What is Theatre?, "The diagnostic of a good drama is that the little it actually displays suggests, like the visible part of an iceberg, larger bulk beneath" (16). If Bentley is correct, as most critics would agree he is, then it seems Camus' major flaw is that his plays tell too much about the iceberg, rather than simply *show* its tip. His tendency toward prolixity about the absurd, and the ethical emphasis upon self-reflection and right action, may account for his commonly attributed title as "existential philosopher."

Nevertheless, the criticism of the untheatrical nature of Camus' plays on stage should not detract from their worth on paper. Without Camus' authentic struggle with the world and his own existence, and the fleshing out of that struggle in words, literary drama would lack some of the great depth of insight into the human situation his plays afford. "The real merit of Camus' theater lies in the sphere of theme rather than form . . . Camus' theater is unequalled for the probity and passion with which it defended human values during a decade in France when they had never been more fragile" (Freeman 164). With fervor, Camus inventively used theatrical forms to portray absurdity and to project lucidity; and through his plays he offered audiences a compelling reason to enact a distinct ethic for living well. The dramatic art that this rhetorical playwright created, in the end, was the kind that few may have enjoyed but most desperately needed.

Works cited

"Albert Camus - Banquet Speech." *Nobelprize.org*. Nobel Media AB 2013. Web. 30 May 2013.

"Albert Camus—Facts." *Nobelprize.org*. Nobel Media AB 2013. Web. 30 May 2013.

Audin, Marie-Louise. "Le paradigme du Théâtre dans Le Mythe de Sisyphe." *Albert Camus et le théâtre: actes du colloque tenu à Amiens en 1988*. Ed. J. Lévi-Valensi. Paris: IMEC, 1992. 105-121. Print.

Bentley, Eric. *In Search of Theater*. New York: Vintage Books, 1959. Print.

---. *What Is Theater?: A Query in Chronicle Form*. Boston: Beacon Press, 1956. Print.

Bree, Germaine. *Albert Camus*. New York: Columbia University Press, 1964. Print.

---. *Camus*. New Brunswick: Rutgers University Press, 1959. Print.

Bronner, Stephen Eric. *Camus: Portrait of a Moralist*. Chicago: University of Chicago Press, 2009. Print.

Camus, Albert. *Caligula and Other Plays*. New York: Penguin Books, 2007. Print.

---. *Caligula. Caligula and Other Plays*. Trans. Stuart Gilbert. New York: Penguin Books, 2007. Print.

---. *Cross Purpose. Caligula and Other Plays*. Trans. Stuart Gilbert. New York: Penguin Books, 2007. Print.

---. *The Just. Caligula and Other Plays*. Trans. Henry Jones. New York: Penguin Books, 2007. Print.

---. *The Myth of Sisyphus and Other Essays*. Trans. Justin O'Brien. New York: Alfred A Knopf, 1961. Print.

---. Preface. *Caligula and Three Other Plays*. Trans. Justin O'Brien. New York: Alfred A Knopf, 1958. Print.

---. *Resistance, Rebellion, and Death*. Trans. Justin O'Brien. New York: Alfred A. Knopf, 1961. Print.

---. State of Siege. *Caligula and Three Other Plays*. Trans. Justin O'Brien. New York: Alfred A Knopf, 1958. Print.

Carroll, David. "Rethinking the Absurd: Le Mythe de Sisyphe." Ed. Edward J. Hughes. *The Cambridge Companion to Camus*. Cambridge: Cambridge University Press, 2007. 53-66. Print.

Corey, Paul. *Messiahs and Machiavellians: Depicting Evil in the Modern Theatre.* Notre Dame: University of Notre Dame Press, 2008. Print.

Cruickshank, John. *Albert Camus and the Literature of Revolt.* New York: Oxford University Press, 1960. Print.

---. Introduction. *Caligula and Other Plays.* By Albert Camus. New York: Penguin Books, 2007. 7-31. Print.

Esslin, Martin. *The Theatre of the Absurd.* Garden City: Anchor Books, 1969. Print.

Freeman, E. *The Theater of Albert Camus: A Critical Study.* London: Methuen and Co. Ltd., 1971. Print.

Genovese, Maria K. "Meaningful Meaninglessness: Albert Camus' Presentation of Absurdism as a Foundation for Goodness." *Pell Scholars* 1 May 2010: 1-14. Digital Commons. Web. 30 May 2013.

Gilead, Amihud. "Plato's Eros, Camus' Sisyphus and the Impossibility of Philosophical Satisfaction." *Clio* 17.4 (1988): 323-344. Print.

Herbeck, Jason. "La fortune scénique de Camus en France: Prise de conscience et mise en scène dans L'État de siège: anatomie d'un échec." Eds. Bastien, Sophie, Geraldine F. Montgomery, and Mark Orme. *La passion du théâtre: Camus à la scène.* New York: Rodopi, 2011. 127-140. Print.

Hoffman, Karen D. "Responses to Despair." *Teaching Philosophy* 27.4 (2010): 337-350. Print.

Kenny, Robert Wade. "The Phenomenology of the Disaster: Toward a Rhetoric of Tragedy." *Philosophy and Rhetoric* 39.2 (2006): 97-124. Print.

Lévi-Valensi, J. "Camus et le théâtre: quelques faits, quelques questions." *Albert Camus et le théâtre: actes du colloque tenu à Amiens en 1988.* Ed. J. Lévi-Valensi. Paris: IMEC, 1992. 13-18. Print.

Moenkemeyer, Heinz. "The Son's Fatal Home-Coming in Werner and Camus." *Modern Language Quarterly* 27.1 (1966): 51-67. Print.

Plato. *Four Texts on Socrates: Plato's "Euthyphro," "Apology of Socrates," "Crito," and Aristophanes' "Clouds."* Cornell University Press, 1998. Print.

Rhein, Phillip H. *Albert Camus.* New York: Twayne Publishers, 1969. Print.

Shakespeare, William. *Hamlet*. New York: Oxford University Press, 2008. Print.

Simpson, Zachary. *Life as Art from Nietzsche to Foucault: Life, Aesthetics, and the Task of Thinking*. Diss. Claremont Graduate University, 2009. Print.

Thody, Philip. *Albert Camus: A Study of His Work*. New York: Grove Press, 1957. Print.

Weddington, Hank S. "The Education of Sisyphus Absurdity, Educative Transformation, and Suicide." *Journal of Transformative Education* 5.2 (2007): 119-133. Print.

Weyembergh, Maurice. *Albert Camus: ou, la mémoire des origines*. Paris: De Boeck Supérieur, 1998. Print.

Zaretsky, Robert. *Camus: Elements of a Life*. Ithaca: Cornell University Press, 2010. Print.

FIGURING CAMUS IN RECENT ALGERIAN WRITING: BETWEEN THE MOTHER AND (IN)JUSTICE

by Joseph Ford

> [L]e problème de notre pays, ce n'est pas la religion, ce n'est pas l'islam. C'est l'injustice.
>
> — HABIB SOUAÏDIA[1]

> J'aime la justice mais j'aime aussi ma mère.
>
> — ALBERT CAMUS[2]

The recent civil war in Algeria, more widely known as the 'decénnie noire' (The Black Decade), may seem an odd occasion to invoke the name of Albert Camus, one of the most celebrated (*French*?) writers of the twentieth century.[3] It may seem even stranger that he occupy

---

[1] *La sale guerre* 330. 'The problem with our country is not religion or Islam. It is injustice.' Translations of cited text to follow in the footnotes; unless stated otherwise, the translations are my own.

[2] Camus reflects on the Nobel Prize giving in a letter to friend and publisher Emmanuel Roblès; see, *Essais* 1843. 'I love justice but I also love my mother.'

[3] Conflict in Algeria erupted following the cancellation of the second round of elections in 1992 in which the FIS (*Front Islamique du Salut*) would have won power. While violence continued into the following decade, it was in 1999, with an amnesty for Islamist fighters (which would equally serve as an amnesty for the Algerian state), that the conflict began to recede. Referred to by some as a 'civil war', many have refuted this label that suits the view of the nationalist 'Pouvoir' who had simply repressed and in some cases fabricated the Islamist enemy.

the work of many of the more famous francophone Algerian authors of the post-independence generation: Salim Bachi, Maïssa Bey, Assia Djebar and Rachid Mimouni are a just a few names among many that establish explicit intertexts with Camus's work. It is perhaps remarkable that it is in Algeria Camus is resurrected – where, in the final years of his life, he had declared a period of silence on the 'question algérienne' that we can almost certainly say occupies the fictional short story 'l'Hôte' ("The Guest"), and where he was widely criticised for his assimilationist position on the French presence in Algeria.[4] While the above-mentioned authors have employed Camus as a ghostly or spectral figure in the contemporary political and social context of Algeria (Kelly), the Algerian-Kabylian exile Alek Baylee Toumi (brother of a current Algerian government minister and feminist activist Khalida Toumi,[5] academic, playwright and poet based in the United States) has himself stuck more rigidly to a specific text and argument of reception concerning Camus's fictional and non-fictional pronouncements on Algeria.[6] Toumi's so-called clarification of 'l'Hôte', *Albert Camus: entre la mère et l'injustice* (*Albert Camus: between the mother and injustice*), with the subtitle "plaidoyer pour la réhabilitation d'Albert Camus en Algérie",[7] offers a dialogical perspective between the conflict of the 1990s and the earlier Algerian War of Independence, as well as taking its place in a developing space of *Algerian* Camus criticism of the twenty-first century.[8]

This article first seeks to demonstrate a general tendency to invoke Camus by figuring him as a hybrid and transcendental figure, straddling the boundaries of fiction and non-fiction, allowing the

---

[4] 'l'Hôte', published in Camus's 1957 collection of short stories, *l'Exil et le royaume*.
[5] Khalida Toumi, previously known as Khalida Messaoudi, is the current Algerian minister for culture.
[6] Christiane Chaulet-Achour has published widely on Camus and contemporary Algeria. See her articles, 'Camus et l'Algérie des années 90' 167-77; 'Camus et l'Algérie. Fraternités littéraires et tensions citoyennes' 13-33; see also her monograph *Albert Camus, Alger*.
[7] 'Plea for the rehabilitation of Albert Camus in Algeria.'
[8] There are two published editions; we refer to one performed and subsequently published in conference proceedings of the group "Les Rencontres méditerranéennes Albert Camus": *Albert Camus et les écritures algériennes: quelles traces* 143-78. In 2012, Toumi published the play as a text in its own right: *Albert Camus: entre la mère et l'injustice*. References to the former edition are henceforth made in body of text.

contemporary writer to challenge official and dominant histories of Algeria. It then considers the potential dangers of the popular and reductive appropriation of Camus's work, questioning the validity of what has been termed a general "Mediterranean lineage" (Gross 131), concluding that Toumi's contemporary work, in its political 'clarification' and adaptation, has in fact not taken account of what Camus sought to do differently across and between the distinct spaces of fiction and non-fiction (Newmark).

In rewriting 'l'Hôte' for the theatre, Toumi attempts to both resurrect a figure of Camus in the context of the Algerian civil war of the 1990s and perform a sort of 'reparative' criticism (Rosello) to repair his reputation in the context of the Algerian War of the 1950s, before his untimely death in 1960. In giving Camus an explicit politics in the adapted play, voiced in the fictional protagonist Daru, the playwright straddles the supposed boundaries of fiction and non-fiction, attacking early postcolonial theorists such as Conor Cruise O'Brien and Edward Said, while simultaneously attempting to recast the ambiguous and ambivalent story of 'l'Hôte', performing the double nature of the title in a multi-directional dialogue across time: the French word 'hôte' translates both as 'host' *and* 'guest', a linguistic *auto-antonym* more commonly known in the Arabic language as 'add'ad'.[9] In addition, and as the title suggests, Toumi addresses the infamous Nobel acceptance speech made by Camus in 1957, where, in response to an interruption from an Algerian student, Camus apparently announces that he will defend his mother before justice (*Ess*, 1882).[10] Toumi's targets, Edward Said, who characterises

---

[9] See Andy Stafford's recent study: 'Ambivalence and ambiguity of the short story in Albert Camus's 'l'Hôte' and Mohammed Dib's 'La Fin'' (220-1). The singular form of 'add'ad' (or ad'dâd') is 'dîd'. Here, with the *auto-antonym* 'hôte', we note an etymological link between the two split meanings; in Latin, the opposing meanings emerge from the same term. It has also been noted that Camus had expressed disappointment that this term could not be translated into English. On these points, see Donald Lazere's anecdotal remarks in *The Unique creation of Albert Camus* (205). The term 'auto-antonym' is presumably derived from Joseph T. Shipley's use of the term 'autantonym' in his 1960 work, *Playing with words*.

[10] Indeed, this incident has subsequently been subject to some controversy in its reporting. The words published in Gallimard's edition of Camus's *Essais*, are recounted by the journalist Dominique Birmann, who worked for *Le Monde* and was present in the room at the time. Since, though, it has emerged that Camus had, in

Camus's work as an unconscious ideological expression of a French colonial sensibility, and O'Brien, who was one of the first critics to consider the 'African' context of Camus's fiction, are furthermore challenged in the 'genèse' published alongside the play, as well as in work published before and since.[11] In an earlier satirical play, *Madah-Sartre*, Toumi also directs criticism at Camus's onetime friend and subsequent enemy Jean-Paul Sartre, reviving him and Simone de Beauvoir in a contemporary Islamist kidnap situation, where Sartre is retrospectively forced to admit that Camus had been right and that he had been wrong on the question of Algeria's future.[12]

Entre la mère et l'injustice is split into four sections: the first two parts effectively replicate Camus's story, the final two continue the story in response to what Toumi has called his need to envisage the fate of the Arab beyond Camus's apparently "unfinished" story (personal correspondence)[13]. The play is effectively a continuation of 'l'Hôte'. In both the first two sections of Toumi's play and the original Camus story, the French settler school-teacher Daru, isolated on the Algerian plateaux at a school cut off in the winter snow, receives an Arab prisoner from a local gendarme, Balducci, who he is directed to deliver to a guard post. Daru, who is reluctant to play a part in the transfer of the Arab to a colonial justice, treats him as an equal, and remaining unwilling to deliver him the following day, leads the prisoner to a crossroads at the mountain, giving him a packet of food and a thousand francs, and offers him a choice to

---

reality, said: "On jette en ce moment des bombes dans les tramways. Ma mère peut se trouver dans un de ces tramways. Si c'est là votre justice, je préfère ma mère à la justice." (Todd 821, citing an interview with the writer C.G. Bjurström) ['At this moment bombs are being planted in the trams in Algiers. My mother could be on one of those trams. If that is justice, I prefer my mother' (Todd 379)] For more on the controversy, see Todd (699-702).

[11] See: Alek Baylee Toumi, 'Albert Camus l'algérian(iste): genèse d'« Entre la mère et l'injustice »' 81-91; 'Albert Camus, l'Algérien: In Memoriam' 88-100. See also, Conor Cruise O'Brien's *Camus* and Edward Said's 'Albert Camus and the French imperial experience', in *Culture and Imperialism* 204-24.

[12] The play was first published in the journal *Algérie littérature/action* (1996) and subsequently translated into English by the author in 2007 with the title, *Madah-Sartre. The kidnapping, trial and conver(sat/s)ion of Jean-Paul Sartre and Simone de Beauvoir*.

[13] In emails exchanged with Alek Baylee Toumi, May 2012.

descend either to prison or to 'freedom' where local tribes would accommodate him (Camus 122-3; Toumi 154-5). As Daru returns to the school, he observes the Arab take the path to the guard post, towards the colonial justice, towards prison. Camus's story ends with Daru discovering an anonymous threat inscribed on the black board of his classroom, which reads: "tu as livré notre frère, tu payeras." (124; 178)[14]

The main adaptation in the first two sections of the play is to be found in the form itself: Toumi replicates much of Camus's style and work in the new play (indeed, Toumi acknowledges Catherine Camus's permission to replicate her father's words in the most recent published version of the play), yet there are a couple of small changes worth mentioning. The first is that Toumi names the infamously nameless Arab. The name Saïd, introduced in the first section, is pronounced around three times throughout the play. Secondly, Camus's *style indirect libre* is lost when translated into direct speech in the play, which removes the sense of ambiguity through the establishment of a univocal narrative voice, losing the omniscient narrator and relying more heavily on unvoiced stage directions. Many gestures and silences are indicated in the stage directions here, which may be more or less visible in the original short story. "DARU *(silencieux)*" is, for instance, inserted by Toumi in the middle of passages of Camus's prose (146) and later where Daru and Balducci argue in the final act (166; 174-5). As Christine Margerrison notes of Camus's own theatre, "some of the greatest strengths of the fictional writings become weaknesses on stage" (68); one cannot help but think of this work as in some ways setting out not only to posthumously rescue Camus's less successful theatre, which had increasingly ignored the needs of the audience in favour of placing the focus on the interpretation of the playwright,[15] but to place Camus himself as a redemptive character within the new play.

Toumi's third section then continues the short story in a dialogue between two new characters, gendarmes Bertini and Fernandez, who having received the Arab at their guard post, ask

---

[14] 'You have delivered our brother, you will pay.'
[15] See Camus's 1958 preface to the US edition of *Caligula*, for instance, in his *Théâtre, Récits, Nouvelles* 1729-34; henceforth *TRN*.

Balducci to return to the school and speak to Daru, who they now suspect of attempting to aid the Arab's escape. Balducci returns in the fourth and final section, where the play presents an extended argument that slips not just between Camus's fictional work and his biography, but, as Toumi puts it in the 'genèse', ends up in a sort of "entre-deux devenu un entre-trois" (91) between a ghostly Camus, a fictional Daru and an autobiographical Toumi.[16] In addition to mentions of "la peste" in Oran and exile to Paris (166), Jacques Cormery, the autobiographical protagonist from Camus's *Le premier homme* (*The First Man*), appears as a journalist who had published troublesome articles on the condition of the Kabylian people under colonial rule – a reference to Camus's 1939 collection of articles 'Misère de la Kabylie' (*Ess* 903-38).[17] Thus, while Toumi claims that it is "Camus [qui] se glisse dans la peau de Daru" (personal correspondence),[18] we become increasingly aware that it is in fact Toumi that figures a slippery version of both Camus and Daru into his own personal narrative surrounding his experience of the latest Algerian conflict. As becomes clear in the 'genèse' to the play, it is Algeria's second war that takes centre stage:

> [...] la passion du théâtre, Américain d'origine kabyle, ni complètement Algérien, ni Français, en exil aux Etats-Unis, dans un entre-deux devenu un entre-trois, la peste galonnée, la barbarie des GIA, nouvelles « misères de la Kabylie » en 2001, ma famille menacée, une sœur condamnée à mort, des islamistes qui sont allés pour égorger ma propre mère à Alger, une seconde guerre d'Algérie qui a déjà fait plus de cent cinquante mille victimes civiles. Si ces morts pouvaient renaître, ne diraient-ils pas tous, à l'unisson, qu'entre ma mère républicaine et la justice intégriste, « je choisirai ma mère avant la justice. » (91)[19]

---

[16] 'a *between two* become a *between three*'

[17] Camus's collection of articles published throughout 1939, 'Misery of Kabylia', would chart the destitution and starvation of the rural Kabylie population of Algeria living and working under colonialism.

[18] 'Camus [who] slips into the skin of Daru'.

[19] '...the passion of the theatre, an American of Kabylian origin, not completely Algerian, nor French, in exile in the United States, in a space 'between two' which

Having set out to 'clarify' Camus's politics, Toumi in reality personalises the politics by figuring himself in the biographical and autobiographical mix. He cleverly maintains a level of ambiguity surrounding the figure of the mother, however: "ma mère républicaine" (republican mother) works both for Camus's mother and the mother Algeria which, on the one hand, becomes the 'république algérienne' (Algerian Republic) of post-independence and, on the other, reverts back to a kind of pre-colonial maternal land-figure. Indeed, Toumi retrospectively reframes the debate on exactly what Camus meant by the mother figure he defended at Stockholm. Thus to see, with Said, "Camus's fiction as an element in France's methodologically constructed political geography of Algeria" (213) is today reframed in a more ambiguous and perhaps purposely ambivalent space; to read the mother as a 'mother France' is now widely viewed as oversimplification. As Assia Djebar writes in *Le blanc de l'Algérie* (*Algerian White*), the very reason she is drawn to Camus's writing, later on in her career, is in this figure of the mother who has remained in Algeria all her life, awaiting the return of Cormery in *Le premier homme*, which is of course her son Camus in real life (31). As for Djebar, so for Toumi, the *Camusian* 'first man' can be seen not as a state of amnesia regarding the colonial past (Wood), but as a state of return to what the Algerian writer Maïssa Bey calls an Algerian "terre-mère";[20] something to which Camus himself alludes in writing *Le premier homme* and which, as Bey tells us, echoes a verse of the Qur'an: "Le paradis est sous les pieds des mères", in Camus's text becomes, "tout homme est le premier homme, c'est pourquoi il se jette aux pieds de sa mere" (Bey, cited in Rice, '"La célébration d'une terre-mère"', 103-4).[21] Thus what had initially been conceived of as a simple recourse to a symbolic metropolitan mother

---

has become a space 'between three', the tasselled plague, the barbarianism of the GIA, new "miseries of Kabylia" in 2001, my family threatened, a sister condemned to death, Islamists who went to slit the throat of my own mother in Algiers, a second Algerian war that has already led to more than 150,000 innocent deaths. If the dead could be reborn, would they not all declare, in unison, that between my republican mother and a fundamentalist justice, "I would choose my mother before justice".'

[20] Roughly translated as 'land-mother'.

[21] 'Paradise lies at the feet of the mother'; 'every man is the first man, this is why he throws himself at the feet of his mother.'

figure must be viewed in more complex terms, as is suggested by more recent writing in this area: as exiled Algerian writers locate "substitute mothers" outside of a patriarchal Algeria (Rice, *Polygraphies* 70-71), so Camus might be seen to locate his substitute mother inside an almost mythical pre-colonial version of Algeria to which his own mother came and never left.[22] Writers such as Bey and Djebar reinforce the active role that can be played by fiction in such contexts; Djebar's oft-noted "fiction comme moyen de « penser »" comes to mind (*Ces voix qui m'assiègent* 233; Harrison).[23]

Toumi's rehabilitation and clarification of Camus's politics is one that encourages a new perspective on memories of the War of Independence, in addition to drawing attention to the interconnectedness of the two ostensibly separate conflicts. Further to the mother/justice question, Toumi's text also revives debates on torture and terror, as well as the founding problems of nationalism. It does so by moving towards a reconfigured postcolonial perspective on Algerian independence, again moving away from the generalist theories of Said. For instance, in what Camus had called a destructive future of the independent Arab state, Toumi now calls problems of "panarabisme" and "panislamisme" during the 1990s (172). The playwright seeks to resituate the historical gaze, placing at least some version of 'Camus' in the contemporary Algerian conflict, no doubt in an attempt to disrupt the old grand narratives of Algerian nationalism at the same time as taking an oppositional stance on the rise of Islamism in Algeria. Toumi endeavours to create a new middle space – a transcendental *third voice* – placing himself at both a generic and political interstices, a position contained in a space of exile, or in a space Camus had defined elsewhere as a 'pensée du midi' or one of 'mesure'.[24] It is now the fictional Daru who voices the contemporary writer's concerns: "Il faudrait une troisième voie, une Algérie plurielle...avec des peuplements fédérés, reliés à la France. Cela me parait préférable à une Algérie liée à un empire islamiste." (172)[25] Whether or not this constitutes 'mesure', or indeed a

---

[22] Camus's mother came to Algeria from Spain and remained there until she died, six months after her son's death.

[23] 'fiction as a way of "thinking"'.

[24] 'Thought at the Meridian', as it is translated in *The Rebel*.

transcendental position on justice, is clearly questionable. Although rereading Camus, we might see some kind of Mediterranean balance in (the new) Daru's statement. While 'mesure' was for Camus a "[m]ère des formes [...] dans le mouvement informe et furieux de l'histoire" (*l'Homme révolté* 372),[26] it remains unclear as to what concrete form this might take in practice.

While, at first glance, his pronouncements in *l'Homme révolté*, of those in power employing the rhetorical pursuit of justice as a means to suppress freedom and civil rights, seem to fit the Algerian context rather well (the FLN's stronghold on power for over 50 years, in the name of a so-called, yet ultimately hijacked, 'independence'[27]), Camus's political philosophy and humanism are by no means unique in this context (LeSueur 110). Again, we ask, why Camus?

Although Toumi's work attacks both sides, in the Islamists and the FLN, any allegiance remains ambiguous and his work could – in "la mère républicaine" – be seen to fall on the side of the nationalists (the new Algerian 'république'), falling short of a *Camusian* 'mesure' and 'pensée du midi' proper. With recent and increasingly prevalent testimony from the Algerian war of the 1990s, which accuses the army of fabricating the Islamist threat – as well as conducting so-called 'false flag' operations (O'Byrne; Samraoui; Souaïdia; Yous) – questions inevitably emerge surrounding the broader complicity of literature itself, both in a potential construction of an orientalised Mediterranean space and in tacitly supporting an oppressive elite, removed from the everyday realities of Algerians. In the worst cases, writers might be said to pedal prevalent nationalist myths, subsuming the official discourse into a dominant social narrative, where writing from the 'status quo' favours one side over the other. The irony, of course, is that the nationalist and Islamist discourses are in many ways dependent on each other and become implosive in a singular space – 'civil war' is perhaps the wrong term to use, in light an ongoing debate over exactly who was killing who (the infamous

---

[25] 'We need a third voice, a plural Algeria...with united populations, linked again to France. That seems to me preferable to an Algeria tied to an Islamist empire.'

[26] 'mother of forms [...] in the formless and furious movement of history'.

[27] The isomorphic narrative of a kind of cyclical colonialism is taken up by Aziz Chouaki in his short article 'Le Tag et le royaume', published in the same edition as Toumi's play (35-40).

'qui tue qui' debate in Algeria). As Camus comments in a 1958 preface to *Caligula*, "on ne peut tout détruire sans se détruire soi-même" (*TRN*, 1729).[28]

In general terms, Camus's rejection of justice in favour of the figure of the mother must, of course, be seen as a practical rejection of an absolute or normative justice, as is apparent from his earlier work in *l'Homme révolté*, where he notes the way in which a justice can preclude a wider implementation of civil rights and individual freedoms:

> Faire taire le droit jusqu'à ce que la justice soit établie, c'est le faire taire à jamais puisqu'il n'aura plus lieu de parler si la justice règne à jamais [...] on confit donc la justice à ceux qui, seuls, ont la parole, les puissants. (359)[29]

With a state-driven post-colonial discourse of re-establishing justice for the Algerian people under the umbrella of a singular nationalism, 'justice', being preserved for those in power, strangles any possibility of rights for the people.

In Camus, Toumi sees that choosing (or preferring) the symbol of the mother over one of 'justice' brings some sort of balance and reconciliation for the Algerian people in return to a pre-colonial vision of the 'terre-mère' over the paternalism and violence of the FLN or Islamist groups. Switching 'justice' for 'injustice' in the title of his work, Toumi performs a certain *auto-antonym*, or Arabic *dîd*, of his own, the two terms becoming almost synonymous in the post-independence context (one term contained within the other), representing the violent indifference of the singular ruling 'Pouvoir' against a supposedly singular, and equally deplorable, 'Islamist' enemy.[30] Recasting the metaphor of *add'ad* blurs and questions the distinction between supposed opposites, performing an important

---

[28] 'One cannot destroy everything without destroying oneself.'

[29] 'To silence the expression of rights until justice is established, is to silence it forever since it will have no more occasion to speak if justice reigns forever [...] we thus confide justice into the keeping of those who alone have the ability to make themselves heard – those in power.'

[30] See Christiane Chaulet-Achour's preface to the most recent edition of the play, 9-12.

function in relation to the aforementioned slippery, perhaps hybrid, space between Islam and post-colonial nationalism – and, ultimately, between 'justice' and 'injustice', which remain to this day unstable categories within and beyond Algeria's borders. Yet, the Arabic *dîf* does not end there; if we are to follow Toumi's logic, and expand the intra- to the extra-textual, we must surely posit that the true ambivalent 'hôte' (host/guest) here is the spectral figure of Camus himself, who sits alongside the (in)justice of post-colonial nationalism and contemporary Islam as a figure of irrevocable ambivalence.

While critics have viewed this kind of theatre as retrospectively 'restorative' and reconciliatory (Gross, citing Rokem), it is perhaps worth observing what the historian of Algeria James D. Le Sueur has called the need for a "retrospective honesty" when it comes to questions of posterity (128). Commenting on Sartre's claim that he had been right to have been be wrong, Rachid Mimouni asks in a 1994 article of Camus and Algeria whether he was wrong to have been right – whether he was wrong to have not known that he was right: "Jean-Paul Sartre, par des pirouettes intellectuelles, avait proclamé qu'il avait eu raison d'avoir tort. Albert Camus aurait-il eu tort de ne pas savoir s'il avait raison?" (14)[31] Fiction, for Camus, was a space in which this sort of tension could be played out; Camus's proposition was one without the certainties of Sartre's historical materialism and it is perhaps this that makes Camus more immediately 'restorative' to Algerian authors today.

Perhaps this is not reparative criticism at all, though. What if Toumi's play takes a step too far, constituting an act of political ventriloquism? To cite Mimouni again, it is the suspended *literary* ambivalence that is central to a Camusian vision of fiction. Witness the following playful and importantly *imaginary* image of Albert Camus:

> S'il nous était possible de le convoquer aujourd'hui pour l'interroger sur l'Algérie [...] je devine ce qu'aurait fait Camus: il aurait allumé une cigarette avant de sortir de son

---

[31] 'Sartre, in an intellectual about-turn, proclaimed that he had been right to be wrong. Was Camus wrong to have not known that he was right?'

> bureau, il aurait longuement marché le long des rues, il
> aurait bu une bière au premier bar rencontré, il aurait
> longtemps humé l'air du temps, souri aux belles dames
> qu'il croisait. Et puis il nous aurait adressé un grand bras
> d'honneur. (ibid.)[32]

Entre la mère et l'injustice attempts to employ contemporary theatre to clarify Camus's non-fiction; in reality, it slips into a non-fictional and biographical (at times *auto*biographical) work. As such, the play could be said to fail to see the difference between literary and political ambivalence in Camus's work. For Camus, fiction was a space where ambivalence constituted a central dynamic; a space within which supposed stable categories of truth and justice could be interrogated. Camus actively does something different, something experimental, within his fiction; as he notes in his philosophical essay, *Le mythe de Sisyphe*: "Les grands romanciers sont des romanciers philosophes, c'est-à-dire le contraire d'écrivains à thèse." (138)[33] In his non-fiction, he is hesitant but clear: the mother, as a human being, comes before a 'justice' which resorted to violence manifested in visible terror (Todd 699-702). One could argue that the overriding point of Camus's 1957 short story – and this is unique to his fiction – is that there is no justice but a colonial justice for the Arab, and that is no justice at all. As Camus had highlighted earlier, to choose between 'victim' or 'executioner' is in fact not to choose at all; the Arab in Camus's story is faced with a choice between 'justice' and 'justice' which results (in a seemingly absurd cycle) in injustice (*Ess* 331-352).[34] It is, then, in fiction that Camus escapes his own

---

[32] 'Were it possible for us to summon Camus today to question him on Algeria [...], I'll take a guess at what he'd say: he'd have lit a cigarette before leaving his office, he'd have walked the streets from end to end, ordered a beer at the first bar he came to, soaking up conversations of the current goings-on, smiling at the beautiful women he passed. Then, he'd have raised his arm in a gesture telling us to get lost.' (The French 'bras d'honneur' is perhaps the UK equivalent of raising one's middle finger.)

[33] 'The great novelists are philosophical novelists, that is to say the opposite of political writers.'

[34] This is perhaps also analogous to the myth of choice regarding the 'coloniser' and the 'colonised'. Both, of course, in many quarters came to be seen as victims of a vicious overarching system of colonialism. Martin Evans and John Phillips cite

personal anxieties about the 'question algérienne', where a level of literary ambivalence and ambiguity can be sustained and quite literally contradict what is said in the non-fiction. While Toumi's political rereading is spot on, his theatre 'continues' Camus's fiction which belies its initial intention: in 'clarifying' Camus's politics by imputing the author's own voice to that of the fictional Daru, the playwright falls into the same trap of the postcolonial critics he accuses of misrepresenting Camus, where no clear distinction is made between the fiction and non-fiction. In other words, the literary ambivalence of the original story is conflated with (what we now know to be) a myth of political ambivalence of the non-fiction. The whole point of 'l'Hôte' is its unfinished nature. Toumi is, though, one among many writers seeking to reinsert the posthumous Camus into contemporary Algerian literature. Others, such as Assia Djebar and Salim Bachi, have (like Mimouni) taken Camus's fictional universe and playfully turned it back on him. In this light, the plurality of Camus's contemporary uses seems to move beyond the invocation of contemporary 'measure' in the context of a violent civil war, beyond the mere restatement of a transcendental justice for all, and towards (or back to) the imaginary spaces of myth and fiction. It is within these imaginative literary modes that notions of truth, justice and freedom – central problems of Camus's philosophy and fiction – are re-interrogated at the level of their incessant and irrevocable ambivalence and ambiguity.

Camus to this same effect at the head of one of their chapters on the recent conflict: 'Algeria's Agony' (177).

Works cited

Bachi, Salim. *Le dernier été d'un jeune homme*. Paris: Flammarion, 2013. Print.

Bey, Maïssa. "Un jour de juin." *Nouvelles d'Algérie*. Paris: Grasset, 1998. Print.

Camus, Albert. *Le mythe de Sisyphe*. Paris: Gallimard, 1942. Print.

---. *l'Homme révolté*. Paris: Gallimard, 1951. Print.

---. *The Rebel*. New York: Knopf, 1954. Print.

---. "l'Hôte." *L'Exil et le royaume*. Paris: Gallimard, 1957. Print.

---. "Misère de la Kabylie" [1939]. *Essais*. Paris: Gallimard, 1965: 903-938. Print.

---. *Essais*. Paris: Gallimard, 1965. Print.

---. *Théâtre, Récits, Nouvelles*. Paris: Gallimard, 1985. Print.

---. *Le premier homme*. Paris: Gallimard, 1994. Print.

---. *The First Man*. London: Penguin, 1996. Print.

Chouaki, Aziz. "Le Tag et le Royaume." *Albert Camus et les écritures algériennes: quelles traces*. Aix-en-Provence: Edisud, 2004. 35-40. Print.

Chaulet-Achour, Christiane. *Albert Camus, Alger*. Biarritz: Atlantica, 1998. Print.

---. "Camus et l'Algérie des années 90." *Europe*, 846 "Albert Camus" (1999): 167-77. Print.

---. "Camus et l'Algérie. Fraternités littéraires et tensions citoyennes." *Albert Camus et les écritures algériennes: quelles traces*. Aix-en-Provence: Edisud, 2004. 13-33. Print.

---. "Préface." Alek Baylee Toumi, *Albert Camus: entre la mère et l'injustice*. Montréal: Editions du Marais, 2012. Print.

Djebar, Assia. *Ces voix qui m'assiègent*. Paris: Albin Michel, 1999. Print.

---. *Algerian White*. New York: Seven Stories Press, 2000. Print.

---. *Le blanc de l'Algérie*. Paris: Albin Michel, 2002 [1995]. Print.

---. *La Disparition de la langue française*. Paris: Albin Michel, 2003. Print.

Evans, Martin and John Phillips. *Algeria: anger of the dispossessed*. London: Yale University Press, 2007. Print.

Gross, Janice. "Albert Camus and contemporary Algerian playwrights: a shared faith in dialogue." *Albert Camus, précurseur: Méditerranée d'hier et d'aujourd'hui*. Ed. Alek Baylee Toumi. New York: Peter Lang, 2009. 127-40. Print.

Harrison, Nicholas. "Assia Djebar: 'Fiction as a way of "thinking"'." *Postcolonial Thought in the French-Speaking World*. Liverpool: Liverpool University Press, 2009. 65-76. Print.

Kelly, Debra. "'An Unfinished Death': the legacy of Albert Camus and the work of textual memory in contemporary European and Algerian literatures." *International Journal of Francophone Studies* 10. 1-2 (2007): 217-35. Print.

Lazere, Donald. *The Unique creation of Albert Camus*. New York: Yale University Press, 1973. Print.

Le Sueur, James D.. *Uncivil War: intellectuals and identity politics during the decolonization of Algeria*. Lincoln: University of Nebraska Press, 2005. Print.

Margerrison, Christine. "Camus and the theatre." *Cambridge Companion to Camus*. Ed. Edward J. Hughes. Cambridge: Cambridge University Press, 2007. 67-78. Print.

Mimouni, Rachid. *La Malédiction*. Paris: Stock, 1993. Print.

---. "Camus et l'Algérie intégriste." *Le Nouvel Observateur* 1544 (1994): 14. Print.

Newmark, Kevin. "Tongue-tied: What Camus's Fiction couldn't teach us about Ethics and Politics." *Albert Camus in the 21st Century: a reassessment of his thinking at a dawn of the new millennium*. Ed. Christine Margerrison, Mark Orme and Lissa Lincoln. Amsterdam: Rodopi, 2008. 107-20. Print.

O'Brien, Conor Cruise. *Camus*. London: Fontana, 1970. Print.

O'Byrne, Myles. *The Front islamique du salut and the denial of legitimacy*. Unpublished PhD thesis, University of Warwick, 2010. Print.

Rice, Alison. ""La célébration d'une terre-mère". Albert Camus et l'Algérie dans les écrits des femmes." *Lendemains* 34. 134-135 (2009): 101-108. Print.

---. *Polygraphies: Francophone women writing Algeria*. Charlottesville: University of Virginia Press, 2012. 86-96. Print.

Rosello, Mireille. *Reparative in narratives: works of mourning in progress*. Liverpool: Liverpool University Press, 2010. Print.

Said, Edward. "Albert Camus and the French imperial experience." *Culture and Imperialism*. London, Vintage, 1994. 204-224. Print.

Samraoui, Mohammed. *Chronique des années de sang. Algérie: comment les services secrets ont manipulé les groups islamistes*. Paris: Denoël, 2003. Print.

Shipley, Joseph T.. *Playing with Words*. N.J.: Prentice-Hall, 1960. Print.

Souaïdia, Habib. *La sale guerre*. Paris: Gallimard, 2001. Print.

Stafford, Andy. "Ambivalence and ambiguity in the short story in Albert Camus's 'l'Hôte' and Mohammed Dib's 'La Fin'." *Postcolonial Poetics: genre and form*. Ed. Patrick Crowley and Jane Hiddleston. Liverpool: Liverpool University Press, 2011. 219-39. Print.

Todd, Olivier. *Albert Camus: une vie*. Paris: Gallimard, 1996. Print.

Todd, Oliver and Benjamin Ivry (trans.). *Albert Camus: a life*. New York. Carroll and Graf, 2000. Print.

Toumi, Alek Baylee. *Madah-Sartre. Algérie littérature/action* 6 (1996). Print.

---. "Albert Camus entre la mère et l'injustice." *Albert Camus et les écritures algériennes: quelles traces*. Aix-en-Provence: Edisud, 2004. 143-178. Print.

---. "Albert Camus, l'algérian(iste): genèse d'« Entre la mère et l'injustice »." *Albert Camus et les écritures algériennes: quelles traces*. Aix-en-Provence: Edisud, 2004. 81-91. Print.

---. *Madah-Sartre. The kidnapping, trial and conver(sat/s)ion of Jean-Paul Sartre and Simone de Beauvoir*. University of Nebraska Press, 2007. Print.

---. "Albert Camus, l'Algérien: In Memoriam." *Nouvelles Etudes Francophones* 25. 2 (2010): 98. Print.

---. "Camus: l'étranger, l'Africain". *Albert Camus aujourd'hui: de l'Etranger au premier homme*. New York: Peter Lang, 2012. 71-84. Print.

---. *Albert Camus: entre la mère et l'injustice*. Montréal: Editions du Marais, 2012. Print.

Wood, Nancy. "Colonial Nostalgia and *Le Premier Homme*." *Vectors of Memory: legacies of trauma in postwar Europe*. Oxford: Berg, 1999. 143-66. Print.

Yous, Nesroulah. *Qui a tué à Bentalha?: chronique d'un massacre annoncé*. Paris: Découverte, 2000. Print.

CAMUS'S ABSURD WORLD AND MEURSAULT'S SUPPOSED INDIFFERENCE

by Mary Gennuso

While most people consider that Meursault in *The Stranger* portrays the indifference required by Camus' concept of the absurd, this paper argues that concept of absurd is a complicated one that evolved over time and that indifference is but one aspect of it. In addition, Meursault does not always display some of the typical indifference assumed of the absurd. In fact, contrary to popular opinion, and Meursault's own contention and persistent retort, he is not as indifferent to his fate as he, or Camus, might have us believe. However, part of the problem of indifference and lack of meaning is couched in the very problematic of the absurd. As we shall see, Camus was not always clear about the meaning of the absurd, and he also somewhat shifted his ideas about this central idea in his later writings. This accounts for some of the difficulty. Another part is the logical conundrums that are raised upon close scrutiny, and that are lodged in the text itself.

The main writings of Camus that are chosen for this endeavor are: *The Myth of Sisyphus and Other Essays (MS), Lyrical and Critical Essays (LCE,)* and, *The Stranger (S)*. The first two are chosen for their philosophical and conceptual detail regarding the absurd, and the third for its literary enactment of the theory. In the first part of this paper we set up a basic framework as we explore the more philosophical aspects of Camus' ideas on the absurd and related concepts, and also make general connections to *The Stranger*. In the second half we look at a few specific episodes in the second half of the novel regarding the main character, Meursault, in order to analyze these concepts and see how they are instantiated in the main figure, along with the conundrums, paradoxes, and problems that are raised through this analysis.

Part I Philosophical Considerations of the Absurd

"The absurd is considered in this essay as a starting point" (*MS* 2). That is, it is a stepping stone and launching point rather than a terminus. In these early essays on the absurd Camus explained this idea in myriad fashion and often connected it with other ideas, building a framework around it. For example, "...in a universe suddenly divested of illusions of lights, man feels an alien, a stranger. [...] This divorce between man and his life, the actor and his setting, is properly the feeling of absurdity" (*MS* 5-6). He then links it to notions of death and suicide. Camus thus asks: "Does its absurdity require one to escape it through hope or suicide. [...] Does the absurd dictate death?" (*MS* 8-9). Camus reiterates this connection. "Reflections on suicide give me an opportunity to raise the only problem to interest me: is there a logic to the point of death? . . . This is what I call an absurd reasoning" (*MS* 9). The problem of suicide is for Camus the "one truly serious philosophical problem" (*MS* 3). While *The Stranger* does not deal with suicide, per se, Camus' writings on suicide touch deeply upon his understanding of death, and hence of life, and how one is to live in the face of such absurdity. Death is an important theme for the absurd and thus *The Stranger* is a story that is intrinsic to the study of Camus' literature as well as his philosophy.

Camus places emphasis on the absurd and thus away from clear meaning and logical analysis. For Camus, even existentialist philosophy was still too hopeful and too logical, given life's absurdity. Perhaps part of this disdain for hope was due to his emphasis on the practical aspects of life. In particular, it is a person's behavior that is important rather than some abstract inner essence that remains out of grasp. Thus Camus writes: "a man defines himself by his behavior as well as by his sincere impulses (*MS* 11)". This philosophy is precisely what we have in *The Stranger* where the main character is of an extremely pragmatic temperament. The novel gives us detailed accounts of his behavior and often the behavior of others. But, how is one to judge what a particular behavior means? Without recourse to intentionality, Camus is hard pressed to provide an answer. Of course, if we can, we can ask the person, or in a novel the narrator might provide the intention. Then the problem becomes if we are to trust the answers given. That is, are the answers provided honest and true answers regarding intentions of behavior? In addition, the matter is more complicated if we ask about psychological factors. Can there be unconscious reasons that are out of the control of the person? Further, there may also be irrational feelings that cannot be easily analyzed. The outburst of feelings, when it does occur, will be extremely important to the story-line of *The Stranger*. These are matters that will be further discussed in our analysis of the novel in the second half of this paper. For now we continue with Camus' conceptual framework. We continue to explore Camus' theory of the absurd.

> But one day the "why" arises and everything begins in that weariness tinged with amazement. "Begins" – this is important. Weariness comes at the end of the acts of a mechanical life, but at the same time it inaugurates the impulse of consciousness. It awakens consciousness and provokes what follows. What follows is the gradual return into the chain or it is the definitive awakening. At the end of the awakening comes, in time, the consequences: suicide or recovery. In itself, weariness has something sickening about it. Here, I must conclude that it is good. For everything begins with consciousness and nothing is worth anything except through it . . . a sketchy reconnaissance in the origin of the absurd. Mere "anxiety" as Heidegger says, is at the source of everything. Likewise, and during every day of an unillustrious life, time carries us. But a moment always comes when we have to carry it . . . Yet a day comes when a man notices or says that he is thirty. Thus he asserts his youth. But simultaneously he situates himself in relation to time. He takes his place in it. He admits that he stands at a certain point on a curve that he acknowledges having to travel to its end. He belongs to time, and by the horror that seizes him, he recognizes his worst enemy.

> Tomorrow, he was longing for tomorrow, whereas everything in him ought to reject it. That revolt of the flesh is the absurd. (But not in the proper sense. This is not a definition, but rather an enumeration of the feelings that may admit of the absurd. Still, the enumeration finished, the absurd has nevertheless not been exhausted). (*MS* 13-14).

Camus here refers to a gradual awakening or consciousness of life that evokes, or is the result of, a certain weariness, or nausea, of the life we are living. When this happens, the person is faced with the prospect of suicide or recovery, or, of course, falling unconscious again, back to the chain, as he says. The point is how he will face his life given this new conscious awareness. This weariness with life is akin to Heideggerian anxiety, to the dulling (and sometimes sharp) angst that permeates our existence. With this awakening comes an awareness of time that brings to the forefront an acknowledgement of what tomorrow will bring, and it brings, ultimately, death. There is a natural "revolt" against this impending future. So the human being, knowing the fate that awaits, is left with the tension of living with the inevitable. The question is again, how does one live out such a life, if the choice is to live at all.

Camus continues regarding the absurd:

> . . . that denseness and that strangeness of the world is the absurd (*MS* 14).

> Likewise this stranger who at certain seconds comes to meet us in a mirror, the familiar and yet alarming brother we encounter in our own photographs is also the absurd (*MS* 15).

> I come at last to death . . . in reality there is no experience of death. Properly speaking, nothing has been experienced but what has been lived and made conscious. Here, it is barely possible to speak of the experience of others' deaths. It is a substitute, an illusion, and it never quite convinces us . . . This elementary and definitive aspect of the adventure constitutes the absurd feeling (*MS* 15).

This strangeness is found especially in relationship and perhaps even the relation to one's own self. One way we recognize this state is by how we perceive or are perceived by others. Our relationship with them has changed. The mark is one of distance. Camus' examples move from the strangeness of the other to the strangeness of the world itself, namely that the human being finds the world a strange place to be in, and this experienced strangeness of the world constitutes another aspect of the absurd, and estranges the self further. For example, Camus utilizes the specific example of the self and the familiar symbol of the mirror, the mirror being an object that can provoke conscious eruption. At such times, on occasion when one glances at a mirror or photograph, one perceives both a familiarity and strangeness in the image. The poignancy of this example is that it illustrates that the ultimate stranger is one's own self. In the final example provided above, the ultimate strangeness is that of the human with respect to death. As Camus says, we cannot really speak of the experience of death since we haven't died yet, and any analysis or expression regarding the deaths of others is somehow substitutive and unconvincing. We may see their dead bodies and know that they were once alive; we may watch them suffer in terrible anguish prior to their death, but we cannot experience their deaths. We cannot know what it is for them. What we experience is our relationship to their passing. What we observe is our own feelings and the meanings are really our own. Often we project our musings on what their life and death was for them. But we never really know their deaths. That is why Camus speaks of the deaths of others as having somewhat of an illusory or even fraudulent quality, since it never really gives us the taste of death.

Death is a prevalent theme for Camus and it will play an important role in *The Stranger* and our analysis of it. There are several deaths in the novel and the reaction of the main character to the deaths of others will also be assessed, especially his relation to his own upcoming death. In the end, though, death provides the ultimate limit to the concept of the absurd since we who are, no longer will be, and what this "no longer will be" really means, escapes us, no matter how much we think about it. Camus comes up with a question regarding death. "Is one to die voluntarily or to hope in spite of everything?" (*MS* 16). But this question is not complete for him. To die voluntarily, is suicide, and that is only one option. Another option that he presents here is: "to hope in spite of everything". However, hope is not something that Camus thinks is the real answer. Still another option is to live without hope. Camus will build up to this point, but first he starts chiseling away at the armor of hope. For example, "That nostalgia for unity, that appetite for the absolute illustrates the essential impulse of the human drama." (*MS* 17).

Thus Camus thinks, like Nietzsche and many others before him (and after him), that any knowledge is only human, perspectival knowledge and not absolute knowledge. Related to this quest for knowledge is a quest for unity, including the quest for unifying principles. This is a type of hope that the universe will make sense and ultimately fits together logically, and even perhaps that it may be based on an absolute principle. Camus echoes sentiments against this type of hope. "We must despair of ever reconstructing the familiar, calm surface which would give us peace of heart" (*MS* 18).

The quest for knowledge leaves us agitated and unfulfilled. Knowledge is a broad term and includes several disciplines. The quest for knowledge, then, leads off to another aspect of strangeness.

> Forever I shall be a stranger to myself. In psychology, as in logic, there are truths but no Truth. "Know thyself" has as much value as the "Be virtuous" of our confessionals . . . They are sterile exercises on great subjects. They are legitimate only in precisely so far as they are approximate (*MS* 19).

Here the strangeness is the strangeness associated with incompleteness and having to settle for approximations of truth and even a plurality of them. This applies as much to psychological truths about the human or about oneself as it does to the outside physical world. Perhaps this is why Camus contents himself with behavioral descriptions of the person, since this is perhaps the only thing that can be got at. In *The Stranger* , the main character often merely describes situations and people. He falls short of analysis. Yet, this does not do away with ambiguity. This lingering ambiguity may yet be another aspect of the absurd. Or, perhaps, it is the desire for clarity that is more absurd.

> This world in itself is not unreasonable, that is all that can be said. But what is absurd is the confrontation of the irrational and the wild longing for clarity whose call echoes in the human heart. The absurd depends as much on man as on the world. . . . It binds them one to the other as only hatred can weld two creatures together . . . (*MS* 21).

> The absurd is essentially a divorce. It lies in neither of the elements compared; it is born of their confrontation . . . The absurd is not in man . . . nor in the world, but in their presence together (*MS* 30).

With these quotes Camus illustrates that absurdity is more in the relationship than in any one thing. In addition, this relationship is, amongst other things, that which exists between the human and the world. Further refined, it is between the irrational forces and a quest for clarity. Even further, the relationship is characterized by hostility. While both of these quotes illustrate the hostile relationship, the first emphasizes the ongoing relationship more than the second since a divorce implies a separation. Interestingly enough, Camus makes a statement that what most binds people together is hatred. This flies in the face of common ideas of love and harmony. Perhaps this is another false hope that Camus wishes us to resist. Camus does not explicate this further, so it is hard to tell how seriously one is to take this point or if it is a polemical argument. In this context, however, it is safe to say that Camus uses it to clarify the agonistic relationship that results in the absurd and in an agitation for the human.

Further, Camus' notion of clarity is not always so clear. In the above context he uses clarity as opposed to the irrational, and seems to imply a human wishing to impose some kind of order or reason on that irrationality. Camus is not always consistent with his terms. We can at least say that he ascribes to a plurality of meanings, to many truths. Therefore, we sometimes have the absurd forces as the irrational, sometimes it is the relationship that is absurd, and sometimes it is the attempt to impose order on that which defies order that is itself absurd. One thing is certain, Camus does think that humans live in tension between opposing pulls. He sums this up again as: "the essential passion of man torn between his urge toward unity and the clear vision he may have of the walls enclosing him" (*MS* 22). In this instance the tug is between a drive to unity, towards perhaps some reasonable principle holding the universe together, a hope perhaps, and a drive towards clarity implying a certain truth and realization of the irrational and of impending walls or doom closing in on one. Yet, a certain paradox ensues. Does not this clarity to see the situation for what it is, to clearly accept the irrational, imply the very use of reason? And, is a unity that excludes the irrational really a unity after all? The divisions are not so clear cut, and perhaps one spills into the other.

Camus' thought takes him always back to death, for, like everything else, "the absurd ends with death" (*MS* 31). This notion of the absurd is so central to Camus' thinking that he says of it: "I judge the notion of the absurd to be essential and consider that it can stand as the first of my truths . . . For me the sole datum is the absurd. [...] I have just defined it as a confrontation and an unceasing struggle." (*MS* 31).

So Camus does have an absolute, or an ultimate value. It is the absurd. In this case Camus calls it the "sole datum". However much truth is relativized, there is still a rock bottom truth. Camus would surely say that his idea of the absurd is not so much based on principle but on pragmatic reality, especially given the reality of death. Yet, however practical this datum might be, it still results in a principle by which he organizes his thoughts.

It is because the absurd defies a clear-cut rationale and especially because it ends in death, or points to death, that Camus says that hope itself must be given up if we are to remain true to reality. To hope would be to falsify existence somehow.

> And carrying this absurd logic to its conclusion, I must admit that that struggle implies a total absence of hope (which has nothing to do with despair) a continual rejection (which must not be confused with renunciation), and a conscious dissatisfaction (which must not be compared to immature unrest). Everything that destroys, conjures away,

> or exorcises these requirements (and, to begin with, consent
> which overthrows divorce) ruins the absurd and devaluates
> the attitude that may then be proposed (*MS* 31).

This is another aspect of why Camus wants to distance himself from the existentialists, especially those of religious persuasion. He finds in them too much logic or reasonableness, and especially, too much hope. Indeed, they even turn the absurd into a religious quest. In MS he reviews the thought of several existentialist thinkers and says of them the following:

> Now, to limit myself to existential philosophies, I see that
> all of them without exception suggest escape. Through an
> odd reasoning, starting out from the absurd of reason, in a
> closed universe limited to the human, they deify what
> crushes them and find reason to hope in what impoverishes
> them. That forced hope is religious in all of them (*MS* 32).

That is, for Camus, the existential philosophers discussed in MS take a wrong turn and even misuse reason to turn the absurd into a hope.

For Camus, for a human being to live authentically amounts to accepting life honestly for what it is and without resorting to false hope or religious crutches. Such a person could live without hope without despairing or committing suicide, and will always "manage". Such a person becomes a type of hero of the absurd in Camus' writings. This is the challenge for the human being, to become conscious in a way that lucidly sees reality in all its absurdity and yet not succumb to hope or despair. To hope is a type of lie one tells oneself to cope with living. This is also why Camus does not put too much stake on finding meaning, since meaning is often fraught with hope. "It was previously a question of finding out whether or not life had to have a meaning to be lived. It now becomes clear, on the contrary, that it will be lived all the better if it has no meaning. Living an experience, a particular fate, is accepting it fully." (*MS* 53). Therefore, the absurd hero lives life fully but without hope. It all depends on how one faces life, which includes how one faces death.

While despair may cause one to commit suicide, the contrary position, he says, "is the man condemned to death", and if one resists the pull to take one's own life, the attitude of this resistance should be "consciousness and revolt" (*MS* 55). By consciousness is implied the proper lucidity to live without hope, and revolt means not apathy, but a certain will in living and thriving despite it all until the bitter end.

> The absurd man can only drain everything to the bitter end, and deplete himself. The absurd is his extreme tension, which he maintains constantly by solitary effort, for he knows that in that consciousness and in that day to day revolt he gives proof of his only truth, which is defiance. This is a first consequence (*MS* 55).

We should therefore expect to see in Camus' literary writing something of this struggle, examples of such awakening, and if handled "well" according to Camus' terms, even a defiance without hope. Since no person knows the hour of their death, it will be hard to "force" this confrontation naturally. The most fitting example, metaphorically, of the death we all have to face, is of some kind of condemned person. *The Stranger* provides just that type of experiment with its story of a condemned criminal. Camus is also concerned with how people use their freedom, particularly in the face of death. Yet, it is not freedom in the abstract as a principle that interests him.

> Knowing whether or not man is free does not interest me. I can experience only my own freedom . . . The problem of "freedom as such" has no meaning . . .

> The only conception of freedom I can have is that of the prisoner or the individual in the midst of the State. The only one I know is freedom of thought and action. (*MS* 56).

If someone is condemned one would think they lose freedom, and Camus does not deny that a certain amount of freedom is lost. In addition, if there is no god or afterlife then gone are "all my chances of eternal freedom". However, there is an increase in "freedom of action" since "that privation of hope and future means an increase in man's availability" (*MS* 57). Hence, this should leave one to live more fully alive in the moment. This is another place where Camus conflates terms for when he says "freedom of action", he often has in mind freedom of thought as well. Sometimes he makes a distinction between the two, but other times not. Nonetheless, it is an important distinction. Otherwise we would have a logical problem. The prisoner, obviously, loses a lot of physical freedom and with it freedom of certain actions. What he still has, though, is freedom of thought.

While the proper response to the absurd is neither hope nor despair, and while it does require a certain amount of will and push towards living life fully, it does, however, paradoxically require, according to Camus, a certain indifference. This indifference is not to be confused with despondency, but is, part and parcel of the acknowledgment merged with revolt.

> The absurd man thus catches sight of a burning and frigid, transparent and limited universe in which nothing is possible but everything is given, and beyond which all is collapse and nothingness. He can then decide to accept such a universe and draw from it his strength, his refusal to hope, and the unyielding evidence of a life without consolation.
> But what does life mean in such a universe? Nothing else for the moment but indifference to the future and a desire to use up everything that is given. Belief in the meaning of life always implies a scale of values, a choice, and our preferences. Belief in the absurd, according to our definitions, teaches the contrary (*MS* 60).

However, even though Camus does not want to acquiesce to a values program, for that would be too much dependant on meaning and perhaps too close to hope, Camus does seem to place a certain value or a certain hierarchy in place precisely because of the absurd in the face of death. Despite his protestation to the opposite, he says: "belief in the absurd is tantamount to substituting the quantity of experience for the quality" (*MS* 60), and again: "what counts is not the best living but the most living" (*MS* 61), and yet still: "there will never be any substitute for twenty years of life and experience" (*MS* 63). Here Camus intends to put the emphasis on the practical.

Therefore he asserts that "value judgments are discarded here in favor of factual judgments" (*MS* 61). His emphasis is very clearly on the sensible and the tangible aspects of life and living. Still, is not to elevate the practical or the tangible to make a value of it? In addition, this quantity over quality seems to conflict with some of Camus' other thoughts that have already been discussed. For example, Camus repeatedly asserts that life must be faced lucidly in the face of the absurd and without hope. This is his type of authenticity. If, therefore, someone approaches life, and death, without this lucidity, or with hope, has not Camus already judged these attitudes with a negative valence? That is, has he not already devalued these responses to the absurd? If so, then it seems that logically, the life faced with lucidity and without hope is clearly of higher value to him than one that might be longer, though false in attitude. So, quality, in this sense of the word, does indeed matter to Camus. The only way he can get out of this bind, at least partially, is to place this comment of quantity over quality within a certain context.

For example, if someone faced with a short life were to use the quality of his life as an excuse, as a way of somehow having hope or rationalizing that his short life was still better than someone else's of longer life, or that it doesn't matter who dies sooner or later since we all have to go anyway, then this might amount to an excuse, an escape, or a hopeful attempted escape from the fate awaited. This is a very slippery slope Camus is on, but this example does warrant some validity. What Camus would want to say here is that even your consciousness of the absurd faced without hope can become a crutch, an escape route, if you fall into thinking that this somehow justifies your life, gives it an unequivocal edge, even if your life ends abruptly. Your life and death must be faced without even the hope of the conscious hopelessness with which you face it. One can see that there is a certain truth in this from Camus' perspective. Indeed, these very arguments will be visited by his main character in *The Stranger* as his death approaches. Still, one cannot help but notice that Camus has gotten himself into a conundrum here. If quantity of life always trumped quality, without any consideration, then there would be no need for lucid consciousness without hope. Camus would probably respond and say that this is not a matter of value but of the truth of existence. Camus clearly places a value on this truth of the absurd and how to face it. His own words seem to elevate, even perhaps at times to glorify, this approach to life.

> Thus I draw from the absurd three consequences, which are my revolt, my freedom, and my passion. By the mere activity of consciousness I transform it into a rule of life what was an invitation to death - and I refuse suicide (*MS* 64).

Strictly speaking, however, Camus does not want to make this an ethic (even if it does have overtones of value), for he says that "the absurd mind cannot so much expect ethical rules at the end of its reasoning" (*MS* 68). It is, rather, that in facing life squarely, and rejecting suicide, an authentic attitude brings with it an acknowledgement of freedom in life, a revolt against wanting to hope and all its implications, and a passion to live life by.

One cannot speak of passionate revolt for Camus without at least briefly mentioning one of his favorite mythic heroes, Sisyphus. Without going into the details of the myth, a few comments of Camus are in order to understand the connection of the myth to the modern individual.

> It is during that return, that pause, that Sisyphus interests me. A face that toils so close to stones is already stone itself! I see that man going back down in a heavy yet measured step toward the torment of which he will never know the end. That hour like a breathing-space which returns as surely as his suffering, that is the hour of consciousness. At each of those moments when he leaves the heights and gradually sinks toward the lairs of the gods, he is superior to his fate. He is stronger than his rock. (*MS* 121)

> The lucidity that was to constitute his torture at the same time crowns his victory. There is no fate that cannot be surmounted by scorn. If the descent is thus sometimes performed in sorrow, it can also take place in joy. (*MS* 121)

These words of Camus unpack his theory and explicate the myth further. The in-between times are times of decision. What is important is that the man continues on, despite knowing the futility of it all. As Camus says, this is his torture, his tragedy, and his crowning glory. Camus adds into this mix an analogy to the modern worker. Camus alluded to this earlier in these essays when he mentioned the daily routine of the worker. There he also brought up the issues of perhaps a point at which consciousness dawns. Here, though, he specifically gives this daily routine of labor the label of the absurd. Camus comes very close here to making a critique of bourgeois labor. However, he does not explicate further. Rather, he insinuates that the same fate awaits today's modern worker. So it is hard to tell if the task itself is meaningless and absurd due to the conditions of modern labor, or if it is in the wider context that Camus is speaking, namely, that death brings or makes an absurd ending to all our undertakings. This condition of the modern worker is one that the main character in *The Stranger* must face, and in that regard he faces the challenge of Sisyphus. In addition, the second half of the novel deals with the character's life in prison and how he will live amidst that daily life. What is important about Sisyphus is that he is victorious because he continues on. In addition, Camus imagines him continuing on happily, not with desperate gloom and doom, but rather with joy. This type of victory and acknowledgement of "happiness" or "joy" is also ascribed to the main character at the end of the novel. It is also the joy of Sisyphus.

> All Sisyphus' silent joy is contained therein. His fate belongs to him. His rock is his thing. Likewise, the absurd man, when he contemplates his torments, silences all the idols. . . . The absurd man says yes and his effort will henceforth be unceasing. If there is a personal fate, there is no higher destiny, or at least there is but one which he concludes is inevitable and despicable. For the rest, he knows himself to be the master of his days. At that subtle moment when man glances backward over his life Sisyphus returning toward his rock, in that slight pivoting he contemplates that series of unrelated actions which become his fate, created by him, combined under his memory's eye and soon sealed by his death. . . . He is still on the go. The rock is still rolling. I leave Sisyphus at the foot of the mountain. One always finds one's burden again. But

> Sisyphus teaches the higher fidelity that negates the gods and raises rocks. He too concludes that all is well. This universe henceforth without a master seems to him neither sterile nor futile. Each atom of the stone, each mineral flake of that night filled mountain, in itself forms a world. The struggle itself toward the height is enough to fill a man's heart. One must imagine Sisyphus happy. (*MS* 122-123)

This long and rather poetic quote from Camus echoes his philosophy of the absurd quite eloquently. The response to the absurd, the proper response for Camus, is the "yes" that is given to life, in spite of it all. It requires consciousness, and is implicated by a certain responsibility for his fate, for Camus points out that although the actions seemed unrelated, they created his fate. In addition, Camus adds the phrase "created by him". So even if there is not an ethics per se in Camus, there is responsibility. As he said earlier in this series of essays:

> All systems of morality are based on the idea that an action has consequences that legitimizes or cancels it. A mind imbued with the absurd never judges that those consequences must be considered calmly. It is ready to pay up. In other words, there may be responsible persons, but there . . . are not guilty ones, in its opinion (*MS* 67).

Thus, while there is responsibility, there is no real "guilt". Therefore, we can expect to see in a character that personifies this attitude, an awareness and acceptance of the circumstances without a feeling of guilt. This will be pivotal in understanding *The Stranger*. Notice, also, that in the previously cited passage, the universe is without a master, namely, without a god, and yet, this does not result in despair, and is neither "servile nor futile". A person can be, in spite of it all, happy amidst the struggle, perhaps even because of it. One final note on this passage and the myth is worth mentioning and that is the amount of earthy and sensory details. Rocks, stones, and physical labor all speak of concrete things, of the tangible world, and it is only with this connection that the jump to the feeling of joy, or of sensory happiness and its contentment, is made, even metaphorically. For the protagonists of Camus' novels, and perhaps for Camus himself, the earthy pleasures are the best, or the most real.

Much has been said, thus far, concerning Camus' concept of the absurd that will be applicable to our nest section on the novel *The Stranger*. Before proceeding with the literary analysis, however, it must be mentioned that in later interviews in 1945 Camus somewhat revised or clarified his position on the absurd.

> Accepting the absurdity of everything around us is in one step a necessary experience: it should not become a dead end. It arouses a revolt that can become fruitful . . . An analysis of the idea of revolt could help us to discover ideas capable of restoring a relative meaning to existence, although a meaning that would always be in danger (*LCE* 346).

This word "absurd" has had an unhappy history and I confess that now it rather annoys me. When I analyzed the feelings of the Absurd in the Myth of Sisyphus, I was looking for a method and not a doctrine. I was practicing methodical doubt. [...] If we assume that nothing has any meaning, then we must conclude that the world is absurd. But does nothing have a meaning? I have never believed that we could remain at this point. Even as I was writing the Myth of Sisyphus, I was thinking about the essay on revolt that I could write later on . . . And then there are newer events that enrich or correct what has come through observation, the continual lessons life offers, which you live and reconsider with those of your earlier experiences. This is what I have tried to do . . . though naturally, I still do not claim to be in possession of any truth (*LCE* 356).

Thus, even Camus concluded that one could not live without some meaning. The clarification that he provides suggests that it was not all meaning that Camus revolted against, but rather meaning steeped in a particular type of hope that Camus considered to be unrealistic, and thus inauthentic, and at bottom, a lie.

Again, in the same book we find an essay entitled "The Enigma", where he further explicates his idea of the absurd, and also revises his position on values quite a bit. He ends up conceding to at least relative values. In addition, there is a certain amount of meaning we give to the world. It is expressed even by the logic of its denial.

> Yet people insist I identify my term or terms, once and for all. Then I object; when things have a label aren't they lost already? (*LCE* 155)

> What is the point of saying again that in the experience which interested me, and which I happened to write about the absurd can be considered as a point of departure –even though the memory and the feel of it still accompany the further advances (*LCE* 159).

Just as there is no absolute materialism, since merely to form this world is already to acknowledge something in the world apart from matter, there is likewise no total nihilism. The moment you say that everything is nonsense you express something meaningful. Refusing the world all meaning amounts to abolishing all value judgments. But living and eating, for example, are in themselves value judgments. You choose to remain alive the moment you do not allow yourself to die of hunger, and consequently you recognize that life has at least a relative value. What in fact does "literature of despair" mean? Despair is silent. Even silence, moreover, is meaningful if your eyes speak. Thus despair is this agony of death, the grave of the abyss. If he speaks, if he reasons, and above all, if he writes, immediately the brother reaches out his hand . . . Literature of despair is a contradiction in terms (159-160).

What is consistent, however, is his "admiration" for a certain type of individual that faces the absurd in the manner already described. While Camus said the following with respect to Prometheus, it could easily apply to Sisyphus.

> At the darkest heart of history, Prometheus men without flinching from this difficult calling, will keep watch over the earth and the tireless grass. In the thunder and lightning of the gods, the chained hero keeps his quiet faith in man. This is how he is harder than his rock and more patient than his culture. His long stubbornness has more meaning for us than his revolt against the gods (*LCE* 142).

In fact, this is the prototype for what he expects from, or sees in, modern man. "One could doubtless claim this God-defying rebel as the model of contemporary man and his protest" (*LCE* 138). It is with this image in mind, and the conglomeration of ideas that Camus has provided us regarding the absurd, that we now move to explore his first, and perhaps most elucidating novel of the absurd, *The Stranger*.

Part II – Is Meursault Really Indifferent to his Impending Death?

Camus' philosophy of the absurd especially takes into account the issue of indifference, and this is a major theme throughout the novel. However, we would contend that along with indifference, there are also episodes where the main character does illustrate a sense of things mattering to him. In the first half of the novel Meursault is particularly indifferent to the women in the novel. He is indifferent to the death of his mother, to marriage to his girlfriend Marie, and indifferent to the unnamed Arab woman whom his friend Raymond beats up and even wants to put her in trouble. However, Meursault does care to please Raymond and even writes a false letter regarding the girl for him. This actually begins the drama that finally ends with the death of the Arab man that Meursault kills on the beach. He cares about enjoying the perks of being part of a couple and enjoying days out on the beach with Masson and Raymond, and enjoying sensual pleasures in general. These are all things that he does care about. In short, the fatal shooting and all that leads up to it has elements of both indifference and caring woven into it.

However, it is the second half of the novel after the shooting that most interests us here. For it is in this second half that the tension between these two opposing poles intensifies acutely, and even exhibits more elements of what he does seem to care about, even if in a negative fashion. For instance, while he does not help his defense much and for the most part participates in his trial as an outside observer wanting merely to state "the facts", he does seem to care a great deal whenever religious themes are mentioned. Early on he gets into a dispute with the magistrate and even heatedly affirms his denial of his belief in God. This seems to matter a great deal to him. He is not indifferent to whether or not there is a God, but any mention of God usually ends up flaring up his anger, as exhibited later in the explosive scene with the chaplain.

Another important element of the second half of the novel involves Meursault's thoughts and introspections while awaiting his execution. We would be amiss if we did not admit that there is some development in his character, for in the second half of the novel Meursault begins to reflect more. It is the Meursault imprisoned who takes notice and remembers. In fact, remembering is one of his pastimes in prison. He remembers events, and he has a good memory of detailing objects. However, we cannot be too quick in saying that Meursault has grown, or that he has had a grand epiphany regarding the importance of feelings or is willing to take responsibility for events.

Imprisoned, Meursault soon realizes that all his musings on escape are futile. But as he says: "one can't be sensible all the time" (S 139). This is quite an odd thing for Meursault to say since for the most part, that is exactly what we learn about Meursault's character. He is sensible at facing reality to a fault. He gets used to things. In addition, aside from momentary hints of feelings welling up, usually angry ones, he shows no emotion. Here the statement regarding not being able to be sensible all the time is probably Meursault's excusing himself for his momentary lapse of facing reality. He does, however, continue to make the best of it. When another day has passed and he realizes that they haven't come for him, he counts his blessings, as one would say.

> Still, I was lucky in one respect, never during any of those periods did I hear footsteps. Mother used to say that however miserable one is, there's always something to be thankful for. And each morning, when the sky brightened and light began to flood my cell, I agreed with her . . . And I knew I had another twenty four hours respite (S 142).

It is still the education that he obtained from his mother that dominates his attitude, even to the bitter end. He still makes the best of it, even pending his execution.

One of the things Meursault contemplates is his appeal, which he first begins by thinking it is denied. He tries to accept this by dwelling on the insignificance of life. So, he reminds himself that "life isn't worth living anyhow", and that the age at which one dies doesn't matter, that eventually dying is inevitable (*S* 143). However, this proves little consolation to him, and is consistent with Camus' general philosophical position, discussed earlier, that quantity of life does matter in an absurd world. Since death does come to all, he argues, "the precise manner of your death has obviously small importance" (*S* 243). In one sense this is true, insofar as death will eventually come regardless. Yet, that is doesn't matter seems an overstatement and a rationalization. Some deaths are more violent than others. In addition, depending on the type of legacy one wants to leave, the reason or type of death, and especially the type of life lived, does matter, even if there is nothing further after death. Finally, though, the purpose of all this reasoning was so that Meursault could follow the rejection of his appeal with the possibility of its acceptance, and thus end up with better thoughts, and as he put it, "earned a good hour's peace of mind" (*S* 144).

Marie also crosses his mind after he is convicted, especially since she has stopped writing. He contemplates the possible reasons. Perhaps she has "grown tired of being the mistress of a man sentenced to death, or she might be ill or dead" (*S* 144). Rather than expressing any sense of loss or emotional let-down, Meursault, again, makes the best of it. His method of doing so, however, is to rationalize and trivialize the relationship. He retorts that "apart form our two bodies, separated now; there was no link between us, nothing to remind us of each other" (*S* 144). That is, now that their bodies can no longer meet and she can't visit and she no longer writes, for all intensive purposes, she no longer exists for him. If she were dead he couldn't have an interest in her and when he is dead people will also forget him. So after all, it seems that mother was right, that "really, there's no idea to which one doesn't get climatized in time" (*S* 144). Meursault is getting used to all his losses and taking them in stride, at least that's how it seems on the outside and from his own statements. Perhaps, however, there is some avoidance mixed in with his cold acceptance.

One of the most significant dialogues takes place during the chaplain's visit. The chaplain forced himself into a meeting with Meursault. When asked about his refusal to see the chaplain,

Meursault answers honestly that he doesn't believe in God. This seems like an incredulous answer to the priest, as it was for the magistrate earlier. Besides, Meursault says, it was a "question of so little importance" (S 145). In what sense is this unimportant? It can only be unimportant since Meursault has to face the death penalty anyway, regardless. Yet, whether or not there is a God and judgment and an afterlife, seems of crucial importance. It is unimportant for Meursault since he has really already rejected the possibility. The priest reacts by leaning back against the wall, the same wall that Meursault leaned against and felt as tangibly sure of as his death sentence, except that the priest now comments that sometimes people aren't as sure as they think. Next the priest inquires whether Meursault feels despair, to which he replies no, just natural fear. The priest tries to befriend Meursault and to get him to ask God for help. He adds that "in his opinion every man on the earth was under sentence of death" (S 146). Meursault responds that it is not the same thing and of no consolation. Yet, the priest has uttered a deep truth as far as existentialism, and even Camus' absurd philosophy, are concerned. Meursault has trivialized the priest's statement because it comes from a priest. He has also pointed out that the only death that interests him is his own, that's why it is of no consolation.

To the bitter end, Meursault remains self-absorbed. He never really contemplates a problem of humankind, but only his own particular distresses. Still, the priest points out, that no matter when someone dies, they still must face "that terrible, final hour" (S 147). He asks a more specific question. "Have you no hope at all? Do you really think that when you die you die outright, and nothing remains?" He replies, "yes" (S 147). The question of hope has been raised and Meursault answers true to the philosophy of the absurd that Camus advocates, without a crutch, that is, without hope. According to Camus, this is admirable, but the idea of an afterlife is not always a matter of hope, for with it often comes the idea of judgment, and hence that it does after all matter how one acted and treated others in this life. On the possibility that there is an afterlife, quite the contrary to what Camus thinks, the thought may not be a crutch but a possibly harsh reality that one will have to face, for not all possibilities of the afterlife are happy ones. Still, neither Meursault nor his author Camus takes up Pascal's wager. One thing is certain, however, and that is that Meursault is by no means indifferent to religious questions. He has very definite ideas and they are not even agnostic but firmly rooted in atheism. That is, his belief is a very strong anti-belief, and this position he cares about a great deal.

The priest continues to badger Meursault, who is getting tired of the discussion, getting bored with it, as he has so many times with others before. The priest's next tactic is to tell him that the real trial isn't this one but that God's justice mattered more, to which Meursault sarcastically replies that it was the former one that condemned him. When the priest brings up the concept of sin, Meursault becomes more adamant.

> I told him that I wasn't conscious of any "sin"; all I knew was that I'd been guilty of a criminal offense. Well, I was paying penalty of that offense, and no one had the right to expect anything more of me (S 148).

The issue of guilt is again raised, however, it is raised in the legal sense that Meursault was found guilty of a crime and that he was paying the price for it, and that was all. The priest, of course, does not think that is all. He refers again to the stone walls and the deep human suffering that they bear witness to, and upon which, sometimes one can see a divine face (S 149). Of course Meursault says he has never seen anything in those stones, not even when he has tried to imagine a face, and the face he tries to imagine is that of Marie, full of desire. The priest wants to elevate the conversation to loftier and spiritual matters and Meursault brings it right back down to earth, where he is comfortable. Notice also that Meursault's imagination is not very good now, and even his memory of Marie seems to fail him. The priest becomes more perturbed and insists, as did the magistrate, that he can't believe Meursault's obstinacy regarding the matter. Meursault, undaunted, says that he will not waste the little time he has left thinking of God. The priest asks one last curious question that really sets off Meursault. He wonders why Meursault has never addressed him as Father, since he is a priest. We are told that the question irritates Meursault, and further, "I told him he wasn't my father" (S 150). Why should this question perturb

Meursault so much? Is it simply because the priest represents a belief system that Meursault does not believe in? Or, has the priest hit a nerve with the mention of "father"? Meursault only has brief memories, given to him by his mother, of his father.

The father is absent in the novel. Meursault may view the priest as a false father substitute that he is not willing to accept. Perhaps also, father means someone who was never around, who left him with too much responsibility, which could account for his having had to give up school. Father, perhaps, means the beginning of having to accept things in life and not dreaming or hoping for a better future. Father, in Meursault's life, may thus even connect to and brings on the absurd, or perhaps is also a limiting factor, signifying death, perhaps morose than the death of the mother. Whatever the reason, Meursault explodes, perhaps even more than on the beach that fatal day when he killed the Arab.

> . . . something seemed to break inside me. I started yelling at the top of my voice. I hurled insults at him, I told him not to waste his rotten prayers on me; it was better to burn than to disappear. I'd taken him by the neck of his cassock, and in a sort of ecstasy of joy and rage, I poured out on him all the thoughts that had been simmering in my brain. He seemed so cocksure, you see. And yet none of his certainties was worth one strand of a woman's hair. Living as he did, like a corpse, he couldn't even be sure of being alive.
> . . . Actually, I was sure of myself, sure about everything, far surer than he; sure of my present life and of the death that was coming. That no doubt, was all I had, but at least that certainty I could get my teeth into just as it had got its teeth into me . . . I'd passed my life in a certain way, and I might have passed it in a different way, if I'd felt like it (S 151)

This passage is quite revealing. First of all, we finally get a full-blown emotional response from Meursault. As one would expect, it is one of rage. This is hardly the response of indifference. He insults the priest and is willing to accept even damnation. Notice his words, "it is better to burn than to disappear". Who has disappeared? Certainly his father has disappeared, and this might be some misplaced aggression towards his absent father. This reference that it is better to burn is also out of place philosophically if one considers that according to the character and author, one does disappear at death, and that to imagine anything, even burning, is a kind of hope in Camus' world, and for Meursault. Thus, this disappearing must speak of something different. We have already mentioned the psychological. On another lever, Meursault's insults are aimed at showing the priest that Meursault, even condemned in jail, is more alive than the priest. The priest, due to his choice of vocation, has spent an existence more disappeared than alive, as indicated also by the reference to being "like a corpse". In addition, the passage goes to enforce Meursault's preference for the tangible and earthly pleasures, and his conviction that these are worth more than abstract spirituality. Meursault says that even one strand of a woman's hair is worth more. The tangible earth and daily life is more certain for Meursault. Finally, the absent father may also be connected to his denial of the existence of God. In most people's minds, and in the Christian theology of his time, God was viewed as the ultimate father figure. Just as his father is absent and will never return, and one should not hope for that impossibility, so one should not hope for an absent God. So goes Meursault's logic.

In addition, Meursault continues that it does not really matter how one spends one's life, that one could have just as easily made other choices. As he says: "nothing, nothing had the least importance" (*S* 152). This, however, seems somewhat contradictory to the speech he has just made where he quite clearly thinks it is better to live his life as he did than as the priest does. He is not <u>that</u> indifferent. The emphasis here, again, is on the ultimate end, death, as being the same regardless, and it is in this vein that indifference is to be the accurate response. Meursault goes even further in his introspection and sounds even more cold-hearted.

> What difference could they make to me, the deaths of others or a mother's love, or his God; or the way a man decides to live, that fate he thinks he chooses, since one and the same fate was bound to "choose' not only me but thousands of millions of privileged people who, like him, called themselves my brothers . . . All alike would be condemned

to die one day; his turn, too would come like the others'. And what difference would it make if, after being charged with murder, he was executed because he didn't weep at his mother's funeral, since it all came to the same thing in the end? The same thing for Salamano's wife and for Salamano's dog. And that little robot woman was as guilty as the girl from Paris who had married Masson, or as Marie, who had wanted me to marry her (*S* 152).

In the above passage, Meursault continues and affirms that since death awaits us all, it really does not matter after all how one lives. Here Meursault adds not only the general and abstract, but the deaths of specific people, like his mother, and that even her death couldn't make a difference to him. How harsh the words that a mother's death does not matter. Yet, this is precisely how Meursault has been acting all the while regarding her death. The comment is meant to point out that no one else's death, not even the death of a mother, can really prepare one for one's own death. Death is something one can only know when one goes through it, and then, ironically, it is not a knowledge that one lives to talk about. Meursault's words also mean that not even a mother or a mother's death can save one from the fate of death. In addition, there is a leveling factor in death that is quite egalitarian, that chooses all regardless of status or wealth or anything else; hence again, it does not matter. Since all are sentenced to die, all are guilty. But, then the priest was right in this regard, wasn't he? We all face a death sentence.

The novel ends on a poetic note, and with further illumination. Again, as the mother's death opened the novel, it comes again to close it.

On the edge of daybreak, I heard a streamer's siren. People were starting on a voyage to a world which ceased to concern me forever. Almost for the first time in many months I thought of my mother . . . and now, it seemed to me I understood why at her life's end she had taken on a fiancé, why she'd played at making a fresh start . . . With death so near Mother must have felt like someone on the brink of freedom ready to start life all over again. No one,

> no one in the world had nay right to weep for her. And I, too, felt ready to start life all over again. It was as if that great rush of anger had washed me clean, emptied me of hope, and, gazing up a that dark sky spangled with its signs and stars, for the first time, the first, I laid my heart open to the benign indifference of the universe. To feel it so like myself, indeed so brotherly, made me realize that I'd been happy, that I was happy still.   For all to be accomplished for me to feel less lonely, all that remained to hope was that on the day of my execution there should be a huge crowd of spectators and that they should greet me with howls of execration (S 153-154).

With death near, a certain release comes, that Meursault describes as freedom. Meursault also seems to make a connection with the immanence of death to being able to face life better, or at least more authentically, more fully, which is a common theme in existential literature. In addition, the release of emotions, in particular the flood of anger that he describes, has enabled Meursault to get rid of any vestiges of hope to which he might have clung. His last images are again of nature, and he accepts, almost defiantly, but at least whole-heartedly, the indifference of the universe. This indifference seems to him now not cold and callous, but brotherly. However, isn't this description of nature also a pull towards the engulfing unity that Camus had warned against in his philosophy? Is this not also a type of act of hope in the cosmic oneness of it all? On the one hand Meursault embraces his fate, looks it squarely in the eye, and yet on the other he still has a pull towards a unity or oneness that Camus ridiculed. Perhaps this is part of what the preoccupation with the senses has been about for Meursault, especially with the ocean swims that he found so enjoyable with Marie. Perhaps nature, and being one with it, has replaced the concept for unity or that of an infinite God that he has rejected.

In addition, there is an ironic twist. He realizes that he had been happy all the while with the little pleasures he enjoyed in his life and that even up to now he was enjoying his life, enjoying whatever little pleasures he had left. However, he didn't need all this introspection to prove that he enjoyed swimming, enjoyed sex with Marie, and enjoyed the sky. There is hidden in his speech a certain mockery of intense reflection and intellectual brooding. What does consciousness buy him after all that he didn't have before? The one thing he does seem to gain is an acute awareness of death and the ability to face it square in the eye (or so he thinks). In addition, his defiant attitude persists to the end in that what he "hopes" for, is that on the day of the execution there will be a crowd of people not weeping for him but hating him. His hope appears ironic, as an anti-hope. However, even this is not so clean and pure as it seems. Throughout the novel Meursault has been reticent and abhorrent towards any display of tender emotions. Yet, he is capable of accepting anger, and even displays it in the dialogue with the priest. So, Meursault cannot face a crowd of weeping people, anymore that he could face the weeping women on the beach. This would make his death somewhat unbearable. In addition, why does he want people there in the end at all? For him to truly be indifferent to his death he should not care if he was alone or with a crowd, if the people cheered or wept, or even if they remained indifferent, like the stones of his prison wall, like the stone-cold beliefs that Meursault holds until the bitter end.

In the end, then, what have we learned about Meursault? He does have an epiphany of sorts regarding the absurdity of life and death. Ironically, though, it is when he is "cornered by death, emptied of hope" that, he finally feels himself freest (*RS* 148). What kind of freedom is this? On the one hand he has lost a lot of physical freedoms, such as smoking, being with a woman, swimming, and just coming and going as he pleases. However, he still has freedom of attitude (*RS* 149). He chooses various ways to cope with his situation, to pass the time remembering all the artifacts in his room, and most of all, he has the freedom to contemplate death. This he does squarely especially when he affirms his disbelief in God to the chaplain. What the confrontation leads to is his affirmation of the life he has lived. Thus the constraint of prison and the confrontation, leads him to a freedom of attitude that is more acute than he previously realized. He becomes more authentic in prison in this regard than he ever was outside of it.

However, if anything, his epiphany serves to confirm the way he has been living all along, not to really change him. He has an even more heightened awareness of life's few pleasures and perhaps more of a gratitude for them, but not much else. More importantly for our purposes, however, is that he was not really indifferent to his fate after all. This is highlighted especially in his reaction to religious discussion and also in the paradoxes and ambiguities that are intrinsic to Camus' logic of the absurd. These are illustrated in the main character especially concerning his last reflections concerning his death. On the one hand he does not despair and takes on the struggle of his life even though he realizes he is facing death. He even displays that rebellious and agonistic attitude that Camus often spoke of in his later writings on the absurd. However, he is clearly not always indifferent to his fate to the point where he even brushes with the fringes of hope, even though it might be a very strong anti-hope after all.

Works cited

Camus, Albert. *L'Etranger*. Edited by Germaine Bree and Carolos Lynes, Jr. Prentice Hall: 1955.

---. *The Myth of Sisyphus and Other Essays*. Edited by Justin O' Brien. New York: Knopf, 1967.

---. *Albert Camus: Lyrical and Critical Essays*. Edited by Philip Thody, translated by Ellen

Conroy Kennedy. New York: Vintage Books, 1970.

---. *The Stranger*. Translated by Stuart Gilbert. New York: Alfred A. Knopf, 1972.

Mauss, Derek C. *Readings on the Stranger*. San Diego: Greenhaven Press, 2001.

ABSURDISM AS SELF-HELP: RESOLVING AN ESSENTIAL INCONSISTENCY IN CAMUS'S EARLY PHILOSOPHY

by Thomas Pölzler

Camus's early philosophy[1] has been subject to various kinds of criticism. It has been said to be nihilistic and dangerous; too vague, or naïve, or simple to be taken seriously; to state personally or historically contingent rather than philosophically significant universal truths; to commit the "is/ought fallacy", and so on. Some of these objections may be warranted, others are clearly flawed, or cannot even be said to be objections at all. In this essay I will address a problem that has not been noticed so far[2]. The problem is that Camus's early philosophy appears to be essentially inconsistent.

As I will try to show in section 1, Camus explicitly denies the existence of moral values. This denial is presupposed by what is probably the most central claim of his early philosophy: his postulation of the absurd. As I will try to show in section 2, Camus is also committed to the existence of certain moral values. Both in his literary and philosophical works he is not so much interested in the absurd *per se*, but rather in how we ought to respond to it (see *Myth* 1, 14; *Caligula*; *Stranger*). In justifying his supposed normative

---

[1] By "early philosophy" I mean Camus's philosophy before around 1943, as it is mainly expressed in the *Myth of Sisyphus*, but also in literary works such as *The Stranger* and *Caligula*.

[2] I briefly mention the problem at the end of my 2011 article on Camus's early "logic of the absurd", see Pölzler 113-114.

conclusions, Camus tacitly, but crucially, relies on evaluative judgements.

If all this is true, then prospects for defenders of absurdism seem bleak. In whichever way the above inconsistency is resolved, they will have to give up or significantly modify central parts of Camus's early philosophy. But things may not stand quite as bad. As I will try to show in section 3, there is a route to consistency that preserves much of Camus's early philosophy, and leaves it *prima facie* plausible. The key is to re-interpret its normative aspects. Stated a bit provocatively, we need to put Camus in the self-help genre.

First Commitment: Moral Values Do Not Exist

Camus's commitment to the non-existence of moral values is rather obvious. At various occasions we find it expressed explicitly. In the *Myth of Sisyphus*, for example, Camus writes: "Belief in the meaning of life always implies a scale of values, a choice, our preferences. Belief in the absurd, according to our definitions, teaches the contrary ... Once and for all, value judgments are discarded here in favour of factual judgments" (*Myth* 58-59). Camus also notes that nobody is guilty (65), and that reasoning cannot be expected to result in ethical rules (66)[3]. Finally, on a more indirect note, he suggests that if they existed, moral values would be closely linked to God (64-65); however, God is an idea that he clearly rejects (65; *Noces*).

As I see it, this nihilism about moral value is entailed by Camus's central postulation of what he calls the absurd. In order to see this, we first have to get clear about what Camus means when he speaks of the absurd. His explanations in the *Myth* tend to be rather vague and diverse; however, we can note at least three basic features that appear to be well-supported by what he says, and upon which most commentators agree[4]. First, Camus sees the absurd as a relation, rather than an object or one-place property. *Two* things must be

---

[3] The non-existence of moral values is a central theme of Camus's early literary work too. Caligula believes that "everything's on an equal footing" (43). According to Meursault, the protagonist of *The Stranger*, nothing makes any difference (41).

[4] For a more detailed explanation of how I understand Camus's conception of the absurd see Pölzler 100-104.

present in order for it to exist. "The absurd is essentially a divorce. It lies in neither of the elements compared ..." (*Myth* 28-29). Second, the relation is supposed to be one of disproportion, contradiction or – as the above quote states – divorce. It arises from a conflict between what we want and what we can realistically hope to achieve. In this sense, Camus believes his notion to be true to our ordinary usage of the term "absurd". "'It's absurd' means 'It's impossible' but also 'It's contradictory.' If I see a man armed only with a sword attack a group of machine guns, I shall consider his act to be absurd. But it is so solely by virtue of the disproportion between his intention and the reality he will encounter, of the contradiction I notice between his true strength and the aim he has in view" (*Myth* 28). And third, the parts of the specific relation of disproportion that Camus is postulating are the subject's quest for meaning on the one hand, and the objective world on the other. Humans essentially strive for unity, intellectual clarity and purpose. But the world is "indifferent" (26), or even "hostile" (13) towards our calls and does not answer them. "At this point of his effort man stands face to face with the irrational. He feels within him his longing for happiness and for reason. The absurd is born of this confrontation between the human need and the unreasonable silence of the world." (*Myth* 26)

Understood in the above way, Camus's postulation of the absurd clearly excludes the existence of meaning. It is not so clear, however, that it also excludes the existence of moral values. Whether it does so depends on what one thinks can confer meaning on our lives. In the *Myth*, and especially in his earliest philosophical essays (*Noces*; *L'Envers*), Camus seems to hold a very ambitious conception of meaning. The only way our "wild longing" could be satisfied, he seems to assume, would be for us to reach perfect and continuous unity (in the sense of being "one" with the world around us, *i.e.*, of losing our subjectivity or the world's losing its objectivity) and perfect and continuous intellectual clarity (in the sense of being able to reduce the world's diverse phenomena to one single explanatory principle). The existence of goodness and badness clearly would not bring about these "impossible"[5] states. Nothing, except from God,

---

[5] In *Caligula* our search for meaning appears to be illustrated by Caligula's quest for the moon. This marks it as a "desire for the impossible" (*Caligula* 40).

could bring them about. Thus, if Camus really held the above conception of meaning, the absurd would appear to be compatible with the existence of moral values.

However, although unity and intellectual clarity are undoubtedly central to his account, it is unlikely that they exhaust it. At various points Camus suggests that the meaninglessness of our lives also arises from our action's lacking a "final purpose" (Pieper 65; Tesak-Gutmannsbauer 10). Consider the following description of the "absurd feeling" of weariness: "Rising, tram, four hours in the office or factory, meal, tram, four hours of work, meal, sleep and Monday, Tuesday, Wednesday, Thursday, Friday and Saturday, according to the same rhythm – this path is easily followed most of the time. But one day the 'why' arises and everything begins in that weariness tinged with amazement" (*Myth* 11). Here the source of our existence's meaninglessness (or at least our feelings of meaninglessness) is supposed to be that we do things for other things' sake, and that we do so on and on and on – but that there isn't anything that would be worth pursuing for itself, and that would thus give our "chain[s] of daily gestures" (*Myth* 11) direction and coherence. Intrinsic moral values could fill this gap. They would be things that are desirable in and of themselves, not just as a means to an end, and would thereby give our lives meaning. Thus, if one believes in the absurd and the meaninglessness by which it is constituted, I think one is committed to the non-existence of moral values after all[6].

That the absurd excludes the existence of moral values is also suggested by some of Camus's explicit remarks about their relation. Recall our above quote from the *Myth*: "Belief in the meaning of life always implies a scale of values, a choice, our preferences. Belief in the absurd, according to our definitions, teaches the contrary." Here Camus explicitly maintains that the absurd is incompatible with any system of values. Moreover, when he states that nobody is guilty and

---

[6] One might worry that this argument only shows the absurd to be incompatible with intrinsic moral value, leaving open the existence of extrinsic such value. However, things can only be valuable because of their contribution to some valuable goal if there actually is any valuable goal. In other words, if nothing is intrinsically valuable, nothing can be extrinsically valuable either.

that there are no ethical rules, he does not just assert so. Rather, he claims that these things *follow from the absurd*: for "a mind imbued with the absurd" nobody is guilty, and reasoning will not result in ethical rules (*Myth* 65, 66).

Second Commitment: Moral Values Exist

Camus's early philosophy seems to be based not only on the denial, but also on the affirmation of moral values. Only few commentators have noticed this second commitment[7]. This is no wonder, given that Camus nowhere explicitly acknowledges that things can be morally better or worse; however, on closer consideration his essays contain lots of evaluative judgements[8]. The things I take Camus to regard as good or praiseworthy are mainly character traits. At various points in the *Myth* he stresses the importance of being lucid, sincere, authentic, courageous and mentally strong, and expresses contempt towards those who lack these virtues. For example, he maintains: "If I become thoroughly imbued with that sentiment that seizes me in face of the world's scenes, with that lucidity imposed on me by the pursuit of a science, I must sacrifice everything to these certainties and I must see them squarely ... Above all, I must adapt my behaviour to them and pursue them in all their consequences" (*Myth* 20). In another noteworthy passage Camus tells us that the discipline, will and clear-sighted struggle exemplified by certain actions "have something exceptional about them" (*Myth* 53)[9].

I also take it that one of the main points of Camus's descriptions of absurd ways of living is to illustrate and further establish the

---

[7] None of these commentators, to my knowledge, has noted the inconsistency to which this gives rise.

[8] One possible objection against my argument in this section would be to claim that making evaluative judgements does not commit one to the existence of moral values. Such judgements are only expressions of emotions, or attitudes, or other conative states. I take this non-cognitivist interpretation of moral language to be generally implausible. Moreover, there is evidence that Camus himself intended his evaluative judgements to actually refer to moral values (see, for example, his commitment to what appears to be some sort a theological voluntarist moral semantics, *Myth*, 64-65, and my remarks at the beginning of section 1).

[9] This interpretation is also defended in Pölzler 111-112.

above virtues. Consider Sisyphus, Camus's most famous example. Sisyphus' condition is supposed to reflect our own absurd fate. Just as humans are "sentenced" to long for meaning without ever being able to achieve it, so Sisyphus is sentenced to the futile labor of anchoring his rock on the top of a mountain. According to Camus's interpretation of the myth, Sisyphus is aware of his tragic condition. But neither does he deceive himself into thinking that he will succeed, nor does he give up and fall into despair. He is lucid, authentic and strong. In fact, in certain moments, Camus thinks, he is even "stronger than his rock" (*Myth* 117, similar points apply to Don Juan, the conqueror and the artist, Camus's other examples of "absurd men").

These considerations already begin to indicate why moral values are essential to the normative aspects of Camus's early philosophy. Before going into detail, however, let us briefly consider which normative claims we are talking about. Suppose you agree with Camus that your condition is absurd. Two natural responses to this recognition are physical, and what Camus calls "philosophical" suicide. If I am aware that regardless of how hard I try, I can never reach what I want most, why should I continue to live at all (Physical suicide)? And if I continue to live, why should I go on actively longing for meaning, knowing that I cannot achieve it anyway? Wouldn't it be wiser to stop doing so, and instead set my hope in God, life after death, reason, or some other idea that transcends existence (Philosophical suicide)? Camus rejects both of these conclusions (*Myth* 29, 48). Instead, he urges us to adopt the mental attitude of "revolt". We ought to acknowledge and maintain the absurd as a fact, but at the same time disapprove of it (take it to be unjust, something that ought not be, a scandal). This means the "total absence of hope", "a continual rejection", and "conscious dissatisfaction" (*Myth* 30). "Living is keeping the absurd alive ... One of the only coherent philosophical positions is thus revolt. It is a constant confrontation between man and his own obscurity. It is an insistence upon an impossible transparency. It challenges the world anew every second. ... That revolt is the certainty of a crushing fate, without the resignation that ought to accompany it" (*Myth* 52).

Camus suggests that what justifies these normative claims is that they conform to demands emanating from the absurd. The absurd requires its being maintained (*Myth* 29). Both physical and philosophical suicide, however, destroy it, for they remove one of the parts of its relation. Being dead, I can no longer strive for meaning. Nor can I if I deliberately stop striving for it. The only way to hold on to the absurd and at the same time express one's legitimate protest against it is to revolt. "The first and, after all, the only condition of my inquiry is to preserve the very thing that crushes me" (*Myth* 29). "There can be no question of masking the evidence, of suppressing the absurd by denying one of the terms of its equation" (*Myth* 48).

To many, this "logic of the absurd" has seemed convincing. On closer consideration, however, it is clearly flawed (see Hochberg 92; Müller-Lauter 125). Camus's postulation of the absurd is a descriptive claim. It informs us about what is the case. But as David Hume has taught us, and as is widely accepted nowadays, no such claim can by itself entail any normative conclusion. In order for a normative conclusion to follow, we also have to appeal to some evaluative standard. This is the point, I think, where Camus's above value judgements come into play. What leads many people to consider his argument sound is not his "logic of the absurd", but rather his implicit appraisal of lucidity, authenticity, courage, and so on. Camus manages to make us aware of the value of these traits. This, and only this (not our belief that the absurd tells us so), is responsible for our tending to agree with his normative conclusions.

At some points the real nature of the argument is not hard to see. For example, in dismissing physical and philosophical suicide, Camus characterizes them as "escape" (*Myth* 30, 34, 50, 52), "evasion" (7), "elusion" (34, 52) or "retreat" (48), and links them to a lack of understanding, to anxiety and helplessness (4, 46, 48). "In a sense, and as in melodrama, killing yourself amounts to confessing. It is confessing that life is too much for you or that you do not understand it" (4). Revolting, in contrast, is taken to be "the contrary of renunciation" (53) and to "give life value" (53).

The Self-Help Resolution

Our above considerations suggest that Camus's early philosophy is essentially inconsistent. Camus is committed not only to the claim that moral values do not exist, but also to the claim that they do. Regardless of how we try to resolve this inconsistency, the theoretical costs will be significant. Giving up the denial of moral values will force us to abandon or modify Camus's central assumption that there is such a thing as the absurd. Giving up the affirmation of moral values will force us to do the same with what Camus mainly argues for in the *Myth*, namely his demands not to commit physical or philosophical suicide, but to revolt. This may lead one to consider absurdism doomed. However, I think there is a way of making Camus's early philosophy consistent that preserves much of its spirit and content, and leaves it *prima facie* plausible.

Camus himself later made the inconsistency disappear by giving up his denial of moral values[10]. In the *Rebel* (13-14) and other essays (in particular *Letters*) he explicitly maintains that human life is worth fighting for, and that we ought to adopt an attitude of solidarity. "The absurd is, in itself, contradiction. It is contradictory in its content because, in wanting to uphold life, it excludes all value judgments, when to live is, in itself, a value judgment" (*Rebel* 16). The emancipation from moral nihilism finds expression in Camus's literary works too. Whereas his earlier novels, plays and literary essays focused on individualistic nihilists such as Meursault or Caligula, he now portrays decent people who put themselves in the service of their community (see in particular *Plague*). Many would say that this makes for a warmer, much more positive philosophy. Defenders of Camus's early views can hardly be satisfied with how he himself resolved his inconsistency, however. Given their close connection to meaning, the affirmation of moral values would force them to concede that our lives might be meaningful after all (which the late Camus indeed seems to acknowledge, *Letters* 28). But this implies that there could be no absurd, or at least not in the sense in which it was originally introduced - and the feeling that there is an

---

[10] Note that Camus's change of mind was not due to worries about consistency, but rather to moral reasons. In the face of, and after World War II, Camus started to feel more and more unease with the radical views expressed in the *Myth*. In his diary he writes, "Consider a thinker who declares: 'Now, I know that this is true. But in the end the consequences repel, and I back off from them.' The truth is unacceptable even for him, who finds it. Thus, we have the absurd thinker with his perpetual anxiety" (1935-1942, own translation).

absurd in this sense is probably what draws most people to Camus's early philosophy in the first place.

The more attractive option for defenders of absurdism seems to be to give up the claim that certain things are valuable. At first sight, this has unacceptable implications too. If one lets go of the idea that it is good to be lucid, authentic, and so on, then Camus's demands not to commit physical or philosophical suicide, but to revolt, seem to have to be regarded as lacking proper support. However, I think there is a way for defenders of absurdism to maintain these claims. They just need to ascribe to them a different (somewhat weaker) status.

Despite his official skepticism about reason, objective truth and philosophy, Camus presents his normative claims in a very strong way. Most naturally, he is read as taking them to hold universally and categorically, *i.e.*, as taking them to be true for all people at all times and places, and regardless of whether they want to conform to them or not. Understood in this way, Camus's demands clearly must be backed up by moral values. But they need not be conceived of in this strong sense. Suppose we read Camus's claims as mere prudential advice. As he sees it, and as many of his readers would agree, the human condition excludes our finding any real meaning. Awareness of this fact can have devastating effects on one's spirits. It can lead to apathy, depression and suicidal tendencies. The point of Camus's early philosophy, on our alternative reading, is to give us self-help style instructions as to how to best cope with our (as it initially seems) tragic condition. Accept the absurd as a fact, defy it as a norm! Exercise the freedom that this change of attitude brings about! Live for the moment, and do nothing for the future! If this is how you live, you will see that there is simply no need to commit suicide or fall into despair. You will still be unable to achieve meaning. But you will yet live a happy and fulfilled life.

On this re-interpretation Camus's demands do not purport to apply to all people at all times and regardless of what they want. They only apply to those who have certain interests. *If* you want to be happy, *then* you ought to revolt, and there is no need for you to commit physical or philosophical suicide. Norms of this hypothetical kind need not be justified by appeal to moral values. That is, the self-help reading allows us to hold on to Camus's demands while at the same time denying the existence of all moral values (even the value of authenticity, lucidity, integrity, and so on).

Of course, this way of resolving Camus's essential inconsistency would only be satisfying if it did not come at the price of making his early philosophy implausible. But I do not think it does. Camus repeatedly stresses that adopting an attitude of revolt allows one to be happy despite the absurd. Remember, for example, the final words of his interpretation of the ancient myth of Sisyphus: "One must imagine Sisyphus happy" (*Myth* 119). Some of us might be able to confirm this from personal experience. But much more importantly, there is also systematically gathered interpersonal evidence suggesting that self-help absurdism might work. According to logotherapy, the deep psychologist school founded by Victor Frankl, consciously choosing an attitude towards things they cannot change helps people to cope with them. It gives them a sense of freedom and superiority (see Frankl). Revolting in the sense of Camus appears to be an exercise of this "defiant power of the human spirit". It may thus indeed be able to help people in general: provide them with a cognitive tool by which they can cope with their absurd destiny, and increase their satisfaction and happiness.

Conclusion

In this essay I have tried to show that Camus's early philosophy is essentially inconsistent. Central parts of his thought presuppose the non-existence of moral values, other central parts their existence. Furthermore, I have tried to show that the best way of resolving this inconsistency is to give up on the existence of moral values altogether, and to re-interpret Camus's demands not to commit physical or philosophical suicide, but to revolt: to read them as self-help rather than as universal and categorical normative judgements.

Some may be dissatisfied with this solution. It might seem to them that reducing them to self-help strips Camus's ideas of the value had by true philosophy. But I do not share this worry. It is certainly not the business of philosophers to provide practical advice on specific matters (such as how to stop smoking in 30 days, or how to lose a certain amount of weight). But there are also problems that concern all of us, regardless of where, when, and how we live. Philosophers have always tried to guide us in our dealings with these problems. I agree with Camus that the absurd is such a problem, and I think that even if interpreted in the suggested way, his advice on how to cope with it is of great philosophical value.

Bibliography

Camus, Albert. "Caligula." *Caligula and Other Plays*. Ed. Albert Camus. Trans. Stuart Gilbert. London: Penguin. 33-104. Print.

---. 'Letters to a German Friend.' *Resistance, Rebellion, and Death: Essays*. Ed. Albert Camus. Trans. Justin O'Brien. New York: Alfred A. Knopf, 1961. 1-32. Print.

---. *L' Envers Et 'Endroit*. Paris: Gallimard, 2005. Print.

---. *Noces*. Alger: Charlot, 1939. Print.

---. *Notebooks 1935-1942*. Trans. Philip Thody. New York: Ivan R. Dee, 2010. Print.

---. *The Myth of Sisyphus*. Trans. Justin O'Brien. London: Penguin, 2005. Print.

---. *The Plague*. Trans. Stuart Gilbert. New York: Vintage, 1991. Print.

---. *The Rebel*. Trans. Anthony Bower. London: Penguin, 1989. Print.

---. *The Stranger*. Trans. Matthew Ward. New York: Vintage, 1989. Print.

Frankl, Viktor E. *Ärztliche Seelsorge - Grundlagen der Logotherapie und Existenzanalyse*. München: Deutscher Taschenbuch Verlag, 2007. Print.

Hochberg, Herbert. Albert Camus and the Ethic of Absurdity.' *Ethics*, 75.2 (1965): 87-102. Print.

Müller-Lauter, Wolfgang. Thesen zum Begriff des Absurden bei Albert Camus.' *Wege der deutschen Camus-Rezeption*. Ed. Heinz R. Schlette. Darmstadt: Wissenschaftliche Buchgesellschaft, 1975. 116-131. Print.

Pieper, Annemarie. *Albert Camus*. München: C.H. Beck, 1984. Print.

Pölzler, Thomas. 'Camus' Early Logic of the Absurd.' *Journal of Camus Studies*, 2011 (2011): 98-117. Print.

Tesak-Gutmannsbauer, Gerhild. *Der Wille zum Sinn*. Hamburg: Dr. Kovac, 1993. Print.

"Camus is Not a Virtue Ethicist: On Sherman's *Camus*"[1]

by Zachary James Purdue

Introduction

David Sherman's 2009 book *Camus* combines excellent scholarship with novel argumentation and methodologies. Sherman's historical overview of Albert Camus's *oeuvre* artfully navigates between being sufficiently controversial to be interesting, on the one hand, and not being so controversial to stray from accepted interpretations, on the other. Very few accounts of Camus's thought in the English language are as ambitious or successful as Sherman's broad overview of Camus's published and unpublished work, filling an important niche in Camus scholarship.

Sherman's *Camus* is at its weakest during its more unique contributions, through which Sherman explains his views on Camus's attempt to formulate an ethics. There are five points of interest in Sherman's argument. First, Sherman tries to establish that Camus initially endorses a traditional virtue ethics. Second, Sherman claims that, during Camus's times, traditional virtue ethics is stripped of its informing background of norms and shared values, and what remains is the individual's ability to see or perceive given

[1] This article contains material from the author's MA thesis, defended Spring Semester 2011 before Kent State Univeristy's Department of Philosophy. The author thanks his advisor, Dr. Linda L. Williams, for the great effort and energies Dr. Williams put forth on the author's behalf, as well as for her invaluable support in formulating and defending these ideas. A more recent version of this article was presented Fall Semester 2013 before Univiersity of South Florida's Philosophy Graduate Student Organzation. The author thanks June Brown for her thorough and deeply helpful commentary on that occasion.

events as moral or amoral. Third, Sherman calls this ability to see events as moral a "phenomenological ethics." Fourth, according to Sherman, Camus builds a new ethics using this "phenomenological ethics" as the foundation. Fifth, and lastly, Sherman calls this new ethics a virtue ethics, albeit a nontraditional one.

The larger version of this paper criticizes all but the second claim; here, in truncated form, the focus is on what is problematic in the claim that Camus espouses a virtue ethics. At points, Sherman successfully demonstrates resonances between Camus's thought and virtue ethics (Sherman 24). However, while Sherman's account gestures at ways in which Camus's thought coheres with certain aspects of virtue ethics, Sherman's account does not support the more robust claim identifying what Camus is doing as virtue ethics. Addressing every step in Sherman's argument would be far beyond the scope of this essay, so herein the focus is on Sherman's "characterological analysis" (Sherman 113) and the degree to which the characterological analysis motivates the claim that Camus is doing virtue ethics.

Sherman attempts a characterological analysis of *The Plague* that considers three characters from *The Plague* and argues that their importance in the novel revolves around three respective "commitments" (explained in greater detail in following sections). These are commitments 1) to happiness in the case of the character Rambert, 2) to understanding in the case of Tarrou, and 3) to the reduction of human suffering in the case of Rieux. Sherman's presentation does not make clear what precise function these characterological analyses and corresponding commitments serve in the overarching argument.

Regarding the characterological analyses, Sherman says "characterological (i.e., individuals with their dispositions of character)" (Sherman 113), which suggests something to do with virtues or vices as habituated states of character—in Aristotle's words, "a state [*hexis*] of character results from [the repetition of] similar activities" (Aristotle 1103b21-22). At another point, Sherman says, "the three principle touchstones of Camus's emerging phenomenological ethics: a commitment to understanding, happiness, and the reduction of human suffering" (Sherman 125), which suggests that the commitments have more to do with the alleged phenomenological move in Camus's ethics. This reading is reinforced here: "I shall analyze the novel's metaphysical, sociohistorical, and characterological themes (the last of which, I shall argue, begins to lay the foundation for what I take to be Camus's developing phenomenological ethics)" (Sherman 113). This reading is inconsistent with Sherman's claim in the following chapter that "virtue ethics reduces to a phenomenological ethics of sorts, and what we are left with...is a bare seeing or perceiving" (Sherman 138), because if all that is left in a phenomenological ethics is this "bare seeing", the characters's commitments would be excluded from this. This quote is helpful, though, for affirming that what Sherman was doing in the prior chapter (the one currently under discussion) was drawing out Camus's virtue ethics. In addition, Sherman says, "the sort of virtue ethics of which I spoke in the last section" (Sherman 133) in the section immediately following the section currently under discussion. Another quote is unhelpful — or at least ambiguous:

> Understanding, happiness, and the diminution of suffering — these are the three primary components of Camus's emerging ethical constellation, and to conclude our consideration of *The Plague*, it is important to make some sense of the ethics that he is offering in it, for there is much in this novel that betokens his later positions, both theoretical...and practical. (Sherman 128)

The meaning of "ethical constellation" is unclear, except for seeming to imply something beyond the "bare seeing" of the phenomenological ethics, and therefore that Sherman is in this section working on Camus's alleged virtue ethics.

Regarding the commitments themselves, the criticisms below deploy in a manner that puts into question this part of Sherman's argument, whether the commitments are virtues or just commitments somehow related to virtue ethics. The convention herein is to use the word "commitments" to preserve the ambiguity until parsing out the possible differences is necessary. The first section — on *The Plague* — explains the characters and corresponding commitments that Sherman identifies. This section problematizes Sherman's methodology by noting what should be, following Sherman's method of characterological analysis, a commitment corresponding to the character Father Paneloux. The next section—on *State of Siege*—explains Sherman's treatment of characters in Camus's *State of Siege* and briefly problematizes Sherman's reading. The conclusion relates the more serious criticisms.

The Plague

Sherman's characterological analysis of characters from The Plague holds water in the sense that the important parts of the plot that revolve around the given characters do apparently focus on these commitments. Many sections of The Plague in which Rieux, the doctor, is the important character tend to highlight the reduction of human suffering, and likewise for Tarrou, the ex-revolutionary, and understanding, and Rambert, the journalist, and happiness. Each is faced with the absurdity of the plague: the plague targets indiscriminately, lasts an indeterminate period, and kills randomly. Its evil is unintelligible, and for these reasons, the plague is difficult to reconcile with moral theory. Each of the characters responds in his special way, often through the commitments just listed. These commitments do not do the characters much good, as none of the commitments provides its patron with a suitable response to the plague. This is appropriate, since the plague is supposed to be an absurd force. For the purposes of the characterological analysis, Sherman does not include a number of other characters who are symbolic of important themes, most notably, Father Paneloux, who is symbolic of the commitment to faith in God, and Cottard, who is symbolic of radical self-interest.

Rieux attempts to reduce human suffering, and his efforts are never clearly effective. Rieux struggles against the plague, lances buboes, administers serum, and so on, but never knows if his victories are because of his work or, rather, just the result of the absurd arbitrary nature of the plague. Possibly, all of his successful interventions only succeed out of pure luck and are not a causal factor in the patients's subsequent recovery. At the beginning of the novel, his wife leaves Oran (the city in which Camus sets the novel) to go to a sanitarium. Throughout the novel, Rieux continuously suppresses his longing for his wife so that his struggle against the plague might be more effective. At the end of the novel, after months of struggle against an opponent with no clear weaknesses, worn out and still missing his wife, when finally the plague is over and Rieux will be able to return to his wife, Rieux finds out his wife has died. Here, the absurd shows itself, as bad things happen to good people *for no discernable reason.*

Tarrou is committed to understanding, worrying about both over- and under-rationalization, and wanting to avoid causing more harm than good in his struggles, be those struggles against the plague or against totalitarianism. However, there is nothing to understand about the plague, or, more specifically, there is nothing that understanding can do against the plague because the plague comes on randomly, strikes randomly, and ends randomly. That is why the plague is such an apt metaphor for the absurd. The plague is nonsensical, and no degree of intellection will solve the problem. As would be expected, Tarrou's alleged commitment to understanding can do virtually nothing against the plague, since by its very nature the plague is not understandable. Tarrou eventually dies of the plague, reinforcing the point that his response, too, cannot win against an absurd foe.

Consider the character Rambert. According to Sherman, Rambert represents the commitment to happiness. Rambert is in Oran by accident, ironically sent there to report on the sanitation conditions that likely contributed to the onset of the plague. Thus, Rambert is not condemned to this fate by any past association with Oran. Rambert is simply stranded there at the onset of the plague, and spends most of the novel trying to escape from the town to pursue happiness in the arms of his lover. However, when Rambert finally gets the opportunity to leave Oran and return to his wife, Rambert chooses not to leave. This represents a change in Rambert's commitment to happiness, from a narrow view to a broader view: "it may be shameful to be happy by oneself" (*The Plague* 184), says Rambert. The question is still open as to precisely whose happiness to be committed, and Sherman does not answer. Nor does Sherman take enough care with the fact that Rambert's conception of happiness changes, though Sherman's methodology relies on an over-all view of Rambert to establish the commitment relevant to

Rambert. This issue is not insurmountable, just problematic if left unattended.

Now, for a more concrete methodological criticism: if Sherman wants his characterological analysis of *The Plague* to be taken seriously as a methodology, and to show that Camus is proposing important commitments (and perhaps virtues), Sherman should be able to answer to problems that arise from extensions of his characterological analysis. As already suggested, the thematic commitment to faith surrounds Father Paneloux. Where others see the plague as a paradigm case for the disproof of God *via* the problem of evil, Paneloux sees the plague as the ultimate call to faith. His commitment to faith requires acceptance of the most despicable "acts of God": "we must hold fast, trusting in divine goodness, even as to the deaths of little children" (*The Plague* 200) Further, Paneloux is working on an essay, the thesis of which is "it's illogical for a priest to call in a doctor" (*The Plague* 202). By this claim, Paneloux is suggesting that, since a priest should have absolute faith in God, a priest should not call a doctor to intervene in an illness since the illness is part of God's plan. Paneloux contracts the plague, refuses to accept treatment (in keeping with his commitment), and, unsurprisingly, dies. Camus, given his atheistic commitments, would not want to promote this sort of faith. However, Sherman offers no justification for the methodological appropriateness of isolating the importance of Rieux, Tarrou, and Rambert's commitments, to the exclusion of other characters and their commitments, e.g. Paneloux and faith.

State of Siege

After Sherman delivers his account of *The Plague*, his analysis switches to one of the plays from Camus's rebellion phase: *State of Siege*. Camus wrote this play after the publication of *The Plague* and the subsequent criticism of the plague's unsuitability as a metaphor for human evil. Instead of conceding to these criticisms, Camus names the main antagonist of *State of Siege* "The Plague." Camus downplays the importance of this choice in the author's preface to *Caligula and Three Other Plays*: "*State of Siege* is in no sense an adaptation of my novel *The Plague*. To be sure, I gave that symbolic name to one of my characters. But since he is a dictator, that appellation is correct" ("Author's Preface" viii). While *State of Siege* is not an adaptation of *The Plague*, the historical importance of naming the antagonist "The Plague" makes *State of Siege* a commentary on *The Plague*, at least in part. The decision signifies that Camus is thumbing his nose at his critics.

Sherman claims that Camus's choice of name here has the significance of denying those criticisms as confusing the message of the novel: "Camus's return to the plague metaphor must be seen as a deliberate refusal to give credence to the types of distinctions that his critics desire to make on the grounds that such distinctions can frequently be used to obfuscate rather than to clarify" (Sherman 132). This is significant in light of Camus's alleged commitment to understanding. Particularly relevant is Tarrou's fear of strong arguments that justify evil acts. The implication is that criticism of the plague's metaphorical aptness hides the importance of Camus's goals in *The Plague*, particularly the importance of trying to do good without recourse to deceptively elegant mental gymnastics, e.g. the kinds of "greater good" arguments used by utilitarians to justify subjugation (Sherman 132-33).

Regarding Diego, the main protagonist in *State of Siege*, Sherman says,

> In broad outline [Diego] seems to transcend both Rieux and Tarrou in the direction of the sort of virtue ethics of which I spoke in the last section... Diego...sets himself to the job of alleviating human suffering as best he can, and...not only ceaselessly reflects on both the limits and requirements of honor but also plainly rejects 'the old argument that to do away with murder we must kill, and to prevent injustice we must do violence' (CTOP, p. 231). (Sherman 133)

This quote is significant not just for indicating, following the section involving the characterological analysis of *The Plague*, that Sherman was talking about virtue ethics in the previous section. Also, the quote announces what, according to Sherman, is something of a refinement of Camus's commitments as put forward in *The Plague*. For Sherman, Tarrou is relevant to *State of Siege* in that Diego,

State of Siege's main protagonist, takes a stance short of Tarrou's wholesale injunction against killing in the sense that Diego does not categorically reject violence (Sherman 133). For Diego, non-violence only holds *prima facie*. This is important to virtue ethics because there are some instances in which killing is the ethically appropriate action. Tarrou's ideological commitments prevent him from choosing to kill even when killing is the right action. This means that there will be situations in which Tarrou cannot but fail to behave in a way that is morally vicious according to the perspective of virtue ethics. Diego stops short of Tarrou's injunction and therefore stops short of committing morally vicious acts by refusing to kill when killing is necessary. In the end, Diego is forced to give up his own life to save the life of his lover, Victoria.

Women have a prominent role in *State of Siege* in the form of a chorus and in particular the character of Victoria. In Sherman's account, Victoria represents progress in the conceptualization of happiness much as Diego represents a step forward from Tarrou's commitments. In *The Plague*, Rambert's commitment to happiness lacks concrete content, at least in the context of Sherman's characterological analysis. Sherman claims that Victoria adds to the account by being the support Diego needs in order to continue his struggle against the Plague (Sherman 134). Without a modicum of happiness, an agent has nothing from which to gain strength in order to make difficult virtuous decisions. This resonates with Tarrou's rhetorical question in *The Plague*: "a man should fight for the victims, but, if he ceases caring for anything outside that, what's the use of his fighting?" (*The Plague* 226)

Victoria criticizes her father, Judge Casado, because Casado uses his legal position as a means of giving vent to his hatred (*State of Siege* 193). Victoria says this results from the fact that Casado has "never loved anything" (*State of Siege* 193). The implication Sherman draws from this is that Casado does not have his modicum of happiness and therefore does not have the support that allows him to make ethical decisions. Casado feels no reason to care, and for that reason does not care.

Sherman claims that Victoria "speaks for the concrete happiness that history has denied for the nominal sake of its realization" (Sherman 134). This refers to the scene immediately preceding

Diego's death, where, after Diego declares his love for Victoria with his "whole soul," Victoria responds, "You loved me with your soul, perhaps, but I wanted more than that" (*State of Siege* 229). Following Diego's death, the chorus of women says, "Curse on [Diego]! Our curse on all who forsake our bodies" (*State of Siege* 229). Sherman thinks that Camus's ethics must be founded in an appreciation for the body: "ethical ideas that lose the body turn against the very impulse that motivated them in the first place" (Sherman 134).

Sherman claims that Victoria "represents the moment of happiness" (Sherman 133) — a concretization of and improvement upon the original commitment as exemplified by Rambert. This seems reasonable. However, applying Sherman's characterological analysis to the context of *State of Siege*, the symbolic value of Diego's sacrifice might be Camus's way of suggesting that the commitments to understanding and the reduction of human suffering are incompatible with the commitment to happiness. Sherman's account could benefit from addressing this.

Concluding Criticisms

Sherman's characterological analysis is problematic for a few reasons, as the above indicates. The section regarding Sherman's treatment of *The Plague* claims that some of these problems result from not extending the method of characterological analysis to other characters or not justifying its restriction to Rambert, Rieux, and Tarrou, as well as from not fully clarifying the analysis in the case of Rambert. The section regarding Sherman's treatment of *State of Siege* suggests that other problems result from not sufficiently considering what the characters's contexts indicate about the characters's allegorical importance and conceptual interrelations. This conclusion considers some broader problems that emerge from Sherman's argument.

First, Sherman owes an account of precisely how and why his argument, including and especially the characterological analyses, demonstrates that Camus is doing virtue ethics. Had Sherman stuck to the less controversial claim that Camus and virtue ethics have certain points of convergence, Sherman would be less vulnerable to this criticism. Second, the metaphor of the plague as an absurd force means there is no account or approach that can somehow deal with the plague. This should also rule out virtue ethics, given that virtue ethics is an approach to promoting human flourishing. In addition to requiring a general response, this latter point significantly magnifies the importance of the former.

Even ignoring the difficulties proposed in the previous two sections, Sherman still owes an account of why commitments to happiness, understanding, the reduction of human suffering, and perhaps Paneloux's faith, are virtues, or at least are suggestive of virtue ethics, in the first place. To gain some perspective on what constitutes a virtue, look to Alasdair MacIntyre's account in *After Virtue*. In Chapter 14, "The Nature of Virtues," MacIntyre attempts to cull from the diverse history of virtue ethics a "unitary core concept of the virtues" (MacIntyre 186). MacIntyre says,

> My account of the virtues proceeds through three stages: a first which concerns virtues as qualities necessary to achieve the goods internal to practices; a second which considers them as qualities contributing to the good of a whole life; and a third which relates them to the pursuit of a good for human beings the conception of which can only be elaborated and possessed within an ongoing social tradition. (MacIntyre 273)

Put briefly, virtues are bound to practice, and contribute to both the individual good and to a contextualized social good, according to MacIntyre. Some of Aristotle's virtues are bravery, temperance, friendliness, and truthfulness (Aristotle 1115a-1127b). Aristotle's temperance, for example, is a virtue even in MacIntyre's sense. Temperance contributes to the individual good by stopping the agent from inappropriately indulging, which in turn contributes to the social good by not wasting resources and by encouraging the appropriate social norms and interactions relevant to ancient Athens.

In this context, how Sherman's account of Camus's commitments could amount to virtues in either the Aristotelian or the MacIntyrean sense is not obvious. Do any of these commitments benefit the individual or social good? Certainly not in the context of *The Plague*, since no single commitment actually has an effect on the plague, protecting neither their patrons nor the society at large. Camus likely did not mean to suggest such commitments are traits that *ought* to be inculcated, since those commitments all necessarily fail given Camus's commitments to absurdity. Why Camus has a virtue ethics to begin with is also unclear, since none of the commitments appear to be virtues.

Granted that there is no identifiable effective approach to take against an absurd force, decisions to act can still bring human meaning and value to an absurd predicament, even in the face of almost certain failure. Sherman could take this route and suggest that Camus is proposing virtue ethics as a way to bring meaning to finite human existence. But why virtue ethics? After his characterological analysis, Sherman attempts to justify why virtue ethics should be the best candidate for how Camus thinks about morality. First, Sherman says, "to make sense of Camus's emerging ethics, we must at least frame it in terms of [contemporary moral] theories" (Sherman 128). Next, Sherman dismisses deontology in a footnote, and explains why Camus would not be a utilitarian. After ruling out the deontological and consequentialist accounts of ethics, Sherman's choice of virtue ethics as a third and last option is more of a default move. Sherman says, "anything like a thorough summary of contemporary moral theories is well beyond what can be undertaken here" (Sherman 128), which is fair. However, apart from virtue ethics, Sherman only compares Camus to two other moral theories, each of which can be shown to be anti-Camusean with little effort. Why not feminine or feminist ethics, or communicative action? Why not any of the less strict re-interpretations of Kant and Mill? Scope is an honest concern, but Sherman's argument suffers severely from failing to inquire seriously into other ethical theories or into what qualifies something as ethical theory and specifically virtue ethics. If Sherman's claim that virtue ethics is a good fit is to stand up, Sherman needs to strengthen his discussion of ethical theory in general.

Sherman tries to approach this problem by suggesting that virtue ethics is already close to Camus because Camus wrote about character. However, just as virtues are at least marginally important to most ethicists, so is character. Consider the case of Immanuel Kant. In *The Grounding of the Metaphysics of Morals*, Kant says,

> There is no possibility of thinking of anything at all in the world, or even out of it, which can be regarded as good without qualification, except a good will. Intelligence, wit, judgment, and whatever talents of the mind one might want to name are doubtless in many respects good and desirable, as are such qualities of temperament as courage, resolution, perseverance. But they can also become extremely bad and harmful if *the will, which in its special constitution is called character*, is not good. (Kant 393, my emphasis)

For Kant, the good will, the only thing "which can be regarded as good without qualification," is based in character. However, Kant is not usually called a virtue ethicist. Why, then, call Camus a virtue ethicist? At least for Kant, the importance of character is explicit. With Camus, the importance of character is announced by an untrustworthy narrator in *The Fall*, and (perhaps) indirectly exhibited by characters from *The Plague*, none of whose character leads to anything resembling triumph over the plague. This section of Sherman's argument fails unless Sherman can offer more evidence demonstrating the importance of character to Camus along with an explanation of why this relates Camus to virtue ethics more than to any other ethical theory concerned with character. Again, how the outlined commitments—to happiness, to understanding, and to the reduction of human suffering—play any role in Sherman's argument toward a Camusean virtue ethics is unclear.

Assuming Sherman could convincingly argue that, for Camus, the commitments to faith, happiness, understanding, and the reduction of human suffering are virtues, and that character plays a role meaningfully similar to its role in virtue ethics, Sherman still has not shown that Camus has a virtue ethics. In other words, the fact that a philosopher talks about virtues and character at some point does not necessarily mean that the philosopher espouses a virtue ethics. The term "virtue ethics" carries a great deal of philosophical tradition. For example, the *Stanford Encyclopedia of Philosophy* says,

> Although modern virtue ethics does not have to take the form known as "neo-Aristotelian," almost any modern version still shows that its roots are in ancient Greek

philosophy by the employment of three concepts derived from it. These are *arête* (excellence or virtue) *phronesis* (practical or moral wisdom) and *eudaimonia* (usually translated as happiness or flourishing). (Hursthouse)

Sherman's analysis falls far short of even these criteria. Realistically, if Camus is a virtue ethicist just because his thought can be interpreted in such a way as to suggest the importance of virtues or character, then so are all other philosophers whose thoughts can be construed in such a fashion.

Of course, there are more ways to attempt to establish that Camus is or is not a virtue ethicist than by holding Sherman's analysis up to Aristotle, MacIntyre, or encyclopedic entries. Similarly, just showing that Sherman's account does not fit the MacIntyrean paradigm would not necessarily rule out Camus's place among any virtue ethicists whatsoever. However, in order to justify the claim that Camus is a virtue ethicist, Sherman needs to advance *some* concrete, identifiable argument, and these sorts of approaches would help. Further, if Sherman is going to talk about Camus as an ethicist at all, Sherman needs to address more rigorously the implications of absurdity for ethical theory and the meaning of ethical theory in the first place. The present author expresses skepticism regarding Camus's place as a virtue ethicist—though not Camus's occasional coherence with virtue ethics—and thinks that Camus's relation to ethics is better construed as metaethical, though not in the sense of contemporary analytic metaethics. This, however, is the topic of a different project upon which the present author is working.

Works cited

Aristotle. *Nichomachean Ethics*. 2nd ed. Trans. Terence Irwin. Indianapolis: Hackett Publishing Company, Inc., 1999. Print.

Camus, Albert. "Author's Preface." Trans. Justin O'Brien. *Caligula and Three Other Plays*. New York: Vintage Books, 1958. v-x. Print.

---. *The Plague*. Trans. Stuart Gilbert. *The Plague, The Fall, Exile and the Kingdom, and Selected Essays*. New York: Everyman's Library, 2004. 1-272. Print.

---. *State of Siege*. Trans. Stuart Gilbert. *Caligula and Three Other Plays*. New York: Vintage Books, 1958. 135-232. Print.

Hursthouse, Rosalind. "Virtue Ethics." *The Stanford Encyclopedia of Philosophy*. Fall 2013 ed. Web. 30 Sept. 2013. <http://plato.stanford.edu/archives/fall2013/entries/ethics-virtue/>

Kant, Immanuel. *Grounding for the Metaphysics of Morals*. 3rd ed. Trans. James W. Ellington. Indianapolis: Hackett Publishing Company, Inc., 1993. Print.

MacIntyre, Alasdair. *After Virtue*. 3rd ed. Notre Dame: University of Notre Dame Press, 2007. Print.

Sherman, David. *Camus*. West Sussex: Blackwell Publishing, 2009. Print.

Meursault (and Caligula) avec de Sade: On the Relations Between the Literary Absurds and Camus's Philosophical Discourses

by Matthew Sharpe

What exactly is the relationship between Camus's analysis of the absurd in *The Myth of Sisyphus* and the fictional "absurds," the drama *Caligula* (1938, then 1944), and *The Outsider* (1941)? And what, more widely, is the relationship between Camus's fiction and his philosophical thought? Why is it that critics can agree that his novels are 'philosophical', at the same time as academic philosophers tend to dismiss him as too literary, or—following Sartre—as a philosophical lightweight?[1] Sartre's remarkable "Explication of the *Stranger*", still arguably one of the astutest responses to *L'Étranger*, at several points approaches a comparatively simple picture that other readers have not failed to develop: "Camus distinguishes, as we have mentioned, between the notion and the feeling of the absurd," Sartre writes: "*The Myth of Sisyphus* might be said to aim at giving us this idea, and *The Stranger* at giving us this feeling."[2] On this reading, Meursault becomes something like an "illustration" of the absurd feeling, and as such, of the philosophical ideas concerning this feeling that Camus developed in *Le Mythe de Sisyphe*, his

---

[1] Jean-Paul Sartre, "Camus' *Outsider*", in *Literary and Philosophical Essays* translated by Annette Michelson (Great Britain: Hutchinson & Co., 1968), 26; Jean-Paul Sartre, "Response to Albert Camus" in *Sartre and Camus: A Historic Confrontation* edited and translated by David A. Spritzen (New York: Humanity books, 2004), 145.

[2] Jean-Paul Sartre, "Camus' *Outsider*", 32.

philosophical essay on the absurd. Sartre can thereby deem *Le Mythe*, in one of its registers, as almost a commentary on *L'Étranger*:

> We are, of course, assured that he is absurd and his predominant characteristic is a pitiless clarity. Besides, he is, in more ways than one, constructed so as to furnish a concerted illustration of the theories expounded in *The Myth of Sisyphus*.[3]

Many readers, whether in enthusiastic sympathy or something closer to moral anxiety, have assumed that Camus must have wanted to present Meursault and/or Caligula as ethical paradigms for new generations to emulate: honest before a godless, chaotic universe. However unlikely the idea seems when stated in direct language, and when we acknowledge the conduct of Albert Camus's own life, we are asked by such readings to see Camus's anomic anti-hero condemned to die for senselessly shooting an Arab ("the only Christ we deserve"[4]), or a crazed theatrical Emperor who dedicates himself to terrorising his own population, as the kinds of amoral existential termini to which Camus's new, post-theological thought would lead us. Hence, to give one example, the eminent philosopher Robert Solomon tells us about *The Outsider* that:

> Meursault is a philosophically fantastic character who, for the first part of the novel, is an ideal Sartrean pre-reflective consciousness, pure experience without reflection … but then, in the second part of the novel [after he is imprisoned and condemned to be executed] … [the] threat of imminent death forces him into a Heideggerian celebration of the

---

[3] Jean-Paul Sartre, "Camus' *Outsider*", 30. Cf. at 28, *Le Mythe* is described as providing "the theory of the novel of absurdity"; at 29, *The Stranger* is a "philosophical translation of his fictional message". Cf. Matthew Lamb, "Re-examining Sartre's Reading of *The Myth of Sisyphus*", *Philosophy Today* 56, 1 (Feb. 2012), 102. But cf. also Sartre, "Camus' *Outsider*", 29-30: :… and Meursault, the hero of *The Outsider*, remains ambiguous, even to the reader who is familiar with the theories of the absurd." Lamb arguably over-simplifies Sartre's review, in order the better to differentiate his own position.

[4] Albert Camus, "Preface to the American edition of *The Outsider*", in Lyrical *and Critical Essays*, 337.

'privilege of death' and the 'happy death' which is a constant theme to Camus' novels ...[5]

Differently, the Christian critic Paul Archambault in *Camus' Hellenic Sources* makes the argument that it is less Meursault than Caligula, hero of Camus's first most successful play, who shows us the truth of Camus's rebellion against metaphysical thought. He sees in Camus's Caligula's crazed longing, after the death of his lover-sister Drusilla, to bring the moon down to earth, make the sun set in the East, and achieve a kind of dark benediction through embracing evil[6] so many proofs that, with Camus, the Church is still confronting avatars of its ancient Gnostic foe. "The gnostic themes of cosmic evil, of liberation through knowledge, and of the need for an initiating teacher" are all present in *Caligula*, Archambault observes. And they are all in his eyes so many "forerunners of modern nihilism," like to that which he sees as characteristic of Camus.[7]

The issue of the precise relation between the different "absurds," as Camus called them[8], continues to divide commentators. For, at the opposite end of the spectrum to Sartre or Archambault, we find positions like that of Thomas Hanna who argues that:

> Those who have tried to make a direct correspondence between the novel and the subsequent philosophical essays succeed only in confusing the proper structure of this novel, which deals with the absurd, but in a manner completely independent of the essays.[9]

Again, Champigny's book on *L'Étranger*, which does not mention *Le Mythe*, is animated by the sense that "Meursault had to be pried from Sisyphus ... [and] a conception of Meursault which was

---

[5] Robert C. Solomon, *Dark Feelings, Grim Thoughts: Experience and Reflection in Camus and Sartre* (New York: Oxford UP, 2006), 16.

[6] Albert Camus, "Caligula", in *Caligula and Other Plays* (London: Pnenguin, 2007), 39-40, 45, 48.

[7] Paul Archambault, *Camus' Hellenic Sources* (University of North Carolina Press: Chapel Hill, 1972), 120, 134.

[8] Albert Camus, *Carnets I. Mai 1935 – Février 1942* (Paris : Les Éditions Gallimard, 1962), 224.

[9] Thomas Hanna, *The Thought and Art of Albert Camus* (Chicago: Regnery, 1958), 55.

still current at the time ...": the idea that he was "a likely personification of the ideas of the absurd formulated in *The Myth of Sisyphus*..."[10] For Matthew Lamb more recently, neither Hanna nor Champigny go far enough in asserting the autonomy of Meursault from Sisyphus, or Camus's novel from his philosophical essay, if that is what we should agree to call *Le Mythe*. Reading *The Myth of Sisyphus* in light of *L'Étranger*, Lamb argues, would show us that Camus was not concerned even in the latter with developing a discursive philosophy. He was writing an ethics. So far is the 1942 essay away from being a commentary or illumination of Meursault's motivations and fate in Camus'famous 1941 novella.[11]

This essay wants to examine, once more, the relationship between Camus's philosophical writings and *L'Étranger* in particular, in the hope of treading a new and "measured," middle ground in these debates. We agree, to some extent, with Lamb and his type of reading which resists seeing Camus's fiction as merely illustrative of a preformed philosophy. As Lamb notes, Camus's explicit resistance to the idea that great literature could ever be like a "thesis-novel", playing out conceptual thought equally expressible in the dispassionate, denotational language of a treatise, needs to be foregrounded in any reflections on this issue.[12] "The thesis-novel, the work that proves, [is] the most hateful of all," Camus writes in *Le Mythe de Sipyphe*, in a tone which is unusually hostile for him. The reason is that it:

---

[10] Robert Champigny, *A Pagan Hero* trans. Rowe Portis (Philadelphia: University of Pennsylvania Press, 1969), 109.

[11] Matthew Lamb, "Re-examining Sartre's Reading of *The Myth of Sisyphus*", 100-111. We leave aside the difficult issue of how an ethics can be written which excludes the philosophical dimension as totally as Lamb is concerned to secure. Certainly, in interview Camus could proclaim: ""*Je ne suis pas un philosophe. Je ne crois pas assez à la raison pour croire à un système. Ce que m'intéresse, c'est de savoir comment il faut se conduire* [what interests me is how it is necessary to conduct oneself]," at Albert Camus, *Albert Camus Oeuvres Complètes II 1944-1948*. (Paris: Gallimard Bibliothèque de la Pléiade: 2006), 659. But it can be disputed whether this excludes the formation of philosophical discourse about possible modes of conduct, as in *Le Mythe*, or instead necessitates it in a thoughtful man like Camus.

[12] Matthew Lamb, "Re-examining Sartre's Reading of *The Myth of Sisyphus*", esp. 107-110.

> ... is ... most often is inspired by a smug thought. You demonstrate the truth you feel sure of possessing ... [Yet] the great novelists are philosophical novelists — that is, the contrary of thesis-writers. For instance, Balzac, Sade, Melville, Stendhal, Dostoevsky, Proust, Malraux, Kafka, to cite but a few ...[13]

Camus's criticism of the idea of the philosophical "thesis-novel" also, we note, underlay his criticism of Jean-Paul Sartre's own first novel, *Nausea*. In this remarkable novel, the young Camus suggested, the "balance" between philosophical ideas and literary creation is "broken." So "the theories do damage to the life."[14] However much the same criticism haunted Camus himself — and can arguably be made of the dramas *Le Malentendu* and *Les Justes*, and his great novel *La Peste* — Camus's hostility towards the idea of novels simply illustrating preformed philosophies should indeed, as Lamb stresses[15], put on our guard against assuming that Camus wanted the fictional absurds to merely illustrate the theoretical notions he developed in *The Myth of Sisyphus*. Then there are more general concerns about identifying an author with any one of his multiple characters, even within a given work. Camus in *L'Étranger* is after all the creator not simply of Meursault, but Raymond, Masson, Marie; Celeste, and *maman*; and in *Caligula* of Caligula but also Cherea, Caesonia, and Scipio etc. Shakespeare is not simply Hamlet, but also the creator of Ophelia, Horatio, and all the other denizens of Hamlet's Denmark, *Cymbeline*'s Cassibulan, and over 30 other settings. To identify an author with any of one of his character, even his heroes, is problematic. On this point, Camus's essay on Roger Martin du Gard gives a revealing insight into Camus's reflections on his own artistic practice:

> A novelist certainly expresses and betrays himself through all of his characters at the same time: each of them

---

[13] Albert Camus, *Le Mythe de Sisyphe* (Paris: Éditions Gallimard, 1942), 137-8.

[14] Albert Camus, "Review of *La Nausée*", in *Lyrical and Critical Essays*, trans. Ellen Conroy Kennedy (New York: Vintage Books, 1970), 199.

[15] Matthew Lamb, "Re-examining Sartre's Reading of *The Myth of Sisyphus*", esp. 107-110.

> represents one of his tendencies or his temptations. Martin
> du Gard is or has been Jacques, just as he is or has been
> Antoine: the words he gives them are sometimes his own,
> sometimes not ...[16]

Nevertheless, "absurd creation" is the header for Part III of *Le Mythe de Sisyphe*, a section wherein Camus goes some way to denying a hard-and-fast distinction between philosophy and literature, as Cruickshank has stressed.[17] Camus certainly numbered *Le Mythe de Sisyphe* alongside *L'Étranger* and *Caligula* in his first cycle of the "absurd," completed on February 21, 1941, as the *Carnets* tells us.[18] *The Myth of Sisyphus* does at one point describe the absurd feeling as involving the sense of oneself a "stranger" in a world "suddenly deprived of illusions and lights." And, whatever else we say about it, something like this feeling (as the novel's title suggests) is the predominant affect of Meursault in the *roman* until the very final scene: a feeling which everywhere until then pervades Meursault's dispassionate, almost bemused, narration of the things that befell him after the unheralded death of *maman*, yesterday or the day before. If any simplistic *"The Stranger* illustrates *The Myth"*-type thesis cannot stand, contra some of Sartre's remarks; then neither will a too strong disavowal of any link between this novel or its contemporary drama *Caligula* and Camus's developing philosophical position. Here as everywhere else, that is, Camus's position is complex or two-sided, and "nothing is true which compels us to exclude."[19]

In order to resolve things more positively, this essay wants — after some further examination of Camus's statements concerning literary art, and his own complex aesthetic make-up (Part 1) — to propose that Camus's Meursault and Caligula do not represent in any way absurd paradigms or ideals: if by that we mean that they should be numbered alongside Don Juan, the actor, conqueror or creator in *Le Mythe*, those "princes without a kingdom" who "know

---

[16] Albert Camus, "On Roger Martin du Gard", in *Lyrical and Critical Essays*, 271-272.
[17] Albert Camus, *Le Mythe*, 132-3; cf. John Cruickshank, *Albert Camus and the Literature of Revolt* (Nw York: Oxford UP, 1959), 143.
[18] Albert Camus, *Carnets I Mai 1935-Février 1942*, 224.
[19] Albert Camus, "Return to Tipasa", in *Lyrical and Critical Essays*, 165.

how to live in harmony with a universe without future and without weakness ..."[20]   In his defence, Sartre does acknowledge this momentarily, when he writes that, had Camus wanted, he might

> ... have related the life of one of those saints of the Absurd, so dear to his heart, of whom he speaks in *The Myth of Sisyphus* ... But he has not done so, and Meursault, the hero of *The Stranger*, remains ambiguous, even to the reader who is familiar with theories of the absurd ...[21]

So what then do we think Meursault and Caligula are doing in Camus's *oeuvre*, if they are not there to illustrate the absurd, or exemplify in literary clothing ideals of lives lived well and truly in face of the absurd?

Our thesis follows, on the one hand, the thread of Camus's comment concerning Roger Martin du Gard, that a writers' characters represent "tendencies or temptations" to which he or she has been subject. It cannot be stressed too much just how much of *The Myth of Sisyphus* and of *L'Homme Révolté* are given over to examining what the first text critiques as metaphorical (or metaphysical) "suicide," and the later text criticises as the metaphysical bases of ideological vindications of murder.[22] This side (or, as it were, either side) of living lucidly with the absurd, *Le Mythe* argues, are those "leaps" which accept either that life *must* have an absolute Meaning, or that it — equally absolutely — *cannot* have any such meaning, outside of forms of irrationalism or fideism.[23] In *The Rebel*, likewise, the *pensée du midi* is a permanent possibility that is hemmed in between forms of absolute affirmation of *le monde, comme il va*, including natural and human evil; and absolute negations of it, which vindicate murder as a righteous protest against the indignities we are made, by God or Nature to endure.[24] The point is that it is very possible that Camus's fictions, if they illustrate any

---

[20] Albert Camus, *Le Mythe*, 126.

[21] Jean-Paul Sartre, "Camus' *Outsider*", 30.

[22] Camus, *Le Mythe*, 17-26; then 48-74; Albert Camus, *L'Homme Révolté* (Paris: Gallimard, 1952), 39-135; 137-313.

[23] Camus, *Le Mythe*, 48-74.

[24] Cf. esp. "Nihilisme et Histoire", in Albert Camus, *L'Homme Révolté*, 131-135.

philosophical notions, have set out to illustrate the "temptation" he wants, ethically, to stage for us but resist: the temptation, for instance, to deify the Irrational like Shestov, Jaspers or Kierkegaard in *Le Mythe*; or the tendency to valorise crime as a form of metaphysical protest, as Camus accuses the romantics and surrealists of doing in *The Rebel*, alongside the Marquis de Sade.[25]

And, with the introduction of Sade, we arrive at the second component to our argument. This component points towards Camus's proximities and distances from the famous pieces written on the tortured Marquis by Adorno and Horkheimer and the great French psychoanalyst, Jacques Lacan.[26] Our hypothesis, put simply, is that Camus in *Caligula* and *L'Étranger* has presented us with characters who embody something very like the irrationalist positions Camus critiques in his important sections of *L'Homme Révolté* devoted to reflecting on how Sade's protest against all order led him, by a strange perversion, to dream up proto-concentration camps given over to the joyless pursuit of sexual joy. While in Caligula's case, the comparison can be made with some directness, we might say that Meursault is more like a "passive Sadean", if this irony can be allowed to stand: less a willing executioner of what too much philosophical and theological *paideia* had allowed him to suppose Nature or God must desire, than unable to keep the murderous Nature carried in the North African sun at bay, when the decisive moment comes, standing on the beach with a gun in his hand.

---

[25] Camus, *Le Mythe*, 53-63; *L'Homme Révolté*, 57-86, 109-130. For Camus's response to André Breton's defence of the romantics, and Camus's reaffirmations of his position, cf. "Révolte et conformisme" and "Révolte et conformisme (suite)", in *Albert Camus Oeuvres Complètes II 1948-1956* (Gallimard Bibliothèque de la Pléiade, Paris: 2008), 392-396.

[26] Theodor Adorno and Max Horkheimer, "Excursus II: Juliette or Enlightenment and Morality", in *The Dialectic of Enlightenment* (Stanford: Stanford UP 2002), 63-93; Jacques Lacan, "Kant with Sade", in in: *Jacques Lacan: Écrits – The first complete edition in English'* translated by Bruce Fink (London: W.W. Norton & Co: 2005), 645-669.

1. Camus's absurd creation: between testimony, myth, and ascesis

The continuing debates concerning the relationship of Camus's art and philosophy of course reflect wider, continuing debates about these two genii of human activity, reaching back to Plato's ruminations on the already "ancient quarrel" of the philosophers with the poets.[27] Camus, at times, disavows that he is a philosopher at all: "Why I am an artist and not a philosopher?", Camus asks himself rhetorically in the *Carnets* of October 1945: "Because I think by words and not by ideas."[28] Yet at times, Camus's disavowals seem less disingenuous than almost ironic, as when he comments that what decides the issue, against his being a philosopher, is that he is interested in how to live: thus reprising *the* Socratic question at the basis of most later antique thought.[29] And, as Cruickshank has commented, *The Myth of Sisyphus'* account of "absurd creation" contains moments where the art-philosophy distinction is almost wholly collapsed, or declared "arbitrary". In an age wherein the possibility of a Spinozist system has been discredited at least, Camus argues:

> ... to anyone who is convinced of the mind's singleness of purpose, nothing is more futile than these distinctions based on methods and objects. There are no frontiers between the disciplines that man sets himself for understanding and loving. They interlock, and the same anxiety merges them ...[30]

Two arguments concerning art run through *Le Mythe*, which are condensed in this important statement. Firstly, taking up the Socratic

---

[27] Plato, *Republic*, 607b.

[28] Albert Camus, *Carnets II, 1942-1951* trans. with Introduction & notes by Philip Thody (London:
Hamish Hamilton, 1966), 73.

[29] "*Je ne suis pas un philosophe. Je ne crois pas assez à la raison pour croire à un système. Ce que m'intéresse, c'est de savoir comment il faut se conduire* [what interests me is to know how we must conduct ourselves]," at Albert Camus, *Albert Camus Oeuvres Complètes II 1944-1948*, 659.

[30] Albert Camus, *Le Mythe*, 132-3; see note 17 above.

interest in how to live, Camus throughout his career will remain reflectively interested in the activity of producing art, as one of the possible ways a person can choose to live their life. A novelist and man of the theatre himself (another of his absurd men is the actor[31]), this is a question dear to his own heart. Whatever an artist may produce, his pursuit of artistic creation for Camus is also a form of "care of the self" or "philosophy as a way of life", to borrow key terms from more recent French thinkers[32]:

> Elsewhere I have brought out the fact that human will had no other purpose than to maintain awareness. But that could not do without discipline. Of all the schools of patience and lucidity, creation is the most effective ... It calls for a daily effort, self-mastery, a precise estimate of the limits of truth, measure, and strength. It constitutes an *ascesis*. All that "for nothing," in order to repeat and mark time! But perhaps the great work of art has less importance in itself than in the ordeal it demands of a man and the opportunity it provides him of overcoming his phantoms and approaching a little closer to his naked reality.[33]

Second is the argument that a specifically "absurd creation" — remembering that not all art is absurd creation, since artists are subject to the same temptations to "escape" as everyone else — can survive the absurd *skepsis* more or less unscathed. The reason is that such art, as opposed to that of the thesis-novelists or artists like Dostoevsky who commit their versions of "philosophical suicide"[34], deigns to explain, so much as to describe, the worlds it fathoms forth

---

[31] Albert Camus, *Le Mythe*, 108-116.

[32] On "care of the self," see for instance *Michel Foucault, The Hermeneutics of the Subject: Lectures at the Collège de France 1981-1982* translated by Graham Burchell (London: Picador, 2005); and Pierre Hadot's *Philosophy as a Way of Life* translated by Michael Chase (London: Wiley-Blackwell, 1996); on Camus's proximity to this conception of philosophy, see M. Sharpe, "Camus' *Askesis*: Reading Camus, in Light of the *Carnets*", *Philosophical Practice*, March 2013, 8.1: 1149-1164; and for a critique from a Christian perspective, Woolfolk, Alan. 1986. "The Artist as Cultural Guide: Camus' Post-Christian Asceticism" *Sociological Analysis*, Vol. 47, No. 2 (Summer 1986), pp. 93-110.

[33] Albert Camus, *Le Mythe*, 155-156.

[34] Cf. Albert Camus, *Le Mythe*, 148-152.

before readers. Absurd art, or art produced by a thinker who wishes to remain true only to what we can know, cling to the concrete: "At a certain point where thought turns back on itself, they raise up the images of their works like the obvious symbols of a limited, mortal, and rebellious thought..."[35] Aware of their inability to totalise the field of human experience, they embrace the sheer diversity of what is given, this side of a total *explanans*:

> Any thought that abandons unity glorifies diversity. And diversity is the home of art. The only thought to liberate the mind is that which leaves it alone, certain of its limits and of its impending end. No doctrine tempts it. It awaits the ripening of the work and of life ...[36]

Camus is here drawing on an entire line of his various philosophical reflections on artistic creation dating back to his earliest published statements and his 1931 encounter in particular with *La Douleur* by André Richaud, Camus was attracted to the model of art as a kind of bearing witness or *témoignage* to all of experience, even experiences usually considered too insignificant to merit polite or philosophical attention. From Richaud, Camus tells us that he learnt that literature could dispense more than forgetfulness or entertainment[37]: "My obstinate silences, this vague but all-pervasive suffering, the strange world that surrounded me, the nobility of my family, their poverty, my secrets — all this, I realised, *could be expressed!*"[38]. An important later Preface to

---

[35] Albert Camus, *Le Mythe*, 136-137.

[36] Albert Camus, *Le Mythe*, 137.

[37] We note that, in his earliest pieces, notably Albert Camus, "Essay on Music," in *Youthful Writings*, trans. Ellen Conroy Kennedy (New York: Alfred A. Knopf, 1976), Camus sees in art a means to escape "the world in which we live with all its horrors": a kind of romantic escapism. But he never returns to this idea, which indeed for him represents the kind of escapist temptation he will setting about rebelling against. (FC 131)

[38] Albert Camus, "Encounters with André Gide", *Lyrical and Critical* Essays, 249. This sense of the artist as bearing witness to even the most abject explains why Camus would take with such warmth to the career of a journalist from 1938. Drawing on his own founding experiences of poverty, it will also inform his continuing sense that artistic creation is always on the side both of political liberty and, contra neoconservative readings of his work, of those humiliated by history's dominant

Chamfort will see Camus holding onto this almost phenomenological sense that "true artists do not scorn anything: they are obliged to comprehend in place of judging," clearly one key dimension of his sense of himself and his role as an artist.[39]

Nevertheless, it is worth noting that, even at the level of this *témoignage*, Camus always challenged the coherence or validity of the idea of art being simply or wholly "realistic". To represent any particular subject involves a choice to represent just that, and nothing else, and to present it in a certain way: so we are dealing with selections and choices. And, as many other aestheticians have noted, re-presenting something in a canvas or poem, by changing its context, alters the ways we perceive it: "I believe I can assert that naturalism is only worthwhile by what it adds to life. Often it idolizes garbage. But this is then no longer just garbage ..."[40] The artist for Camus, even when she counts herself a realist, is not in the business of recreating reality. She must some way re-present it, by selecting particular aspects and images from the fabric of experience which s/he elevates to a different, symbolic or representative status.[41] By themselves, the important early essay "Art in Communion" explains, even the beauty of Mediterranean evenings (so dear to Camus) has but "a dreamy and sterile insignificance." Art's "more certain light" selects and represents aspects and elements of this unfolding, fleeing experience.[42] It is as if art in this way enacted a kind of "pause" — almost photographically, in a way which evokes similar ideas in Walter Benjamin[43] — capturing the fleeting sense of an

---

powers.

[39] Camus cited at Monique Crochet, *Les Mythes dans L'Oeuvre d'Albert Camus* (Paris: Éditions Universitaires, 1973), 224.

[40] Albert Camus, "Art in Communion," in *Youthful Writings*, 219.

[41] Cf. Albert Camus, *L'Homme Révolté*, 320-321.

[42] Albert Camus, "Art in Communion", in *Youthful Writings*, 222.

[43] Albert Camus, "Art in Communion", 216, 223. A decade before Camus, Walter Benjamin had developed similar reflections about art in the age of mechanical reproduction (for instance, of images in photography) as devolving now towards "exhibition value", as against its more traditional "ritual value". Benjamin at times seems to hold out the hope that now art, shorn from the task of producing beautiful, auratic semblances, can begin to explore new means of play, as anticipated or glimpsed in the play of children; or else, as for instance in Walter Benjamin, "The Little History of Photography" *Selected Writings Volume II* translated by M. W.

experience: not by penetrating to "what lies beneath the delicate world of gesture and form," but through the artist's "giving oneself to it and communicating with it ..."[44]

In contrast to what we are given in *The Myth of Sisyphus*, however, there is both in Camus's literary works of the 1940s in particular, and in his continuing reflections on aesthetics, a very different strand that holds onto art's pedagogic or psychagogic role. For the Camus of this tendency, artists should not let go of the old Platonic idea that it is artists who "create the decisive myths for our conduct," even if they are not as Shelley or Nietzsche suggested, the often unacknowledged legislators of the world.[45] He rails in "The Enigma" against the romantic idea that artists should be thought to write solely about themselves in these terms: "It is not wholly excluded, on the contrary, that an artist be interested at base in others, or in his times, or in [certain] familiar myths," Camus protests in "The Enigma".[46] Reflecting upon his own artistic creation in the first two cycles of his production, Camus thus can comment in the *Carnets* that he was "without doubt and until now ... not a novelist in the widely accepted sense. Above all [I am] an artist who creates myths to the measure of his passion and of his anguish ..."[47] It is not for nothing that *The Myth of Sisyphus* bears the title it does and concludes with the famous section wherein Camus almost completely reframes this classical *mythos* in an affirmative way that horrified Blanchot, for one.[48] As Crochet (and more recently, Ronald

---

Jephcott and K. Shorter (Cambridge: Cambridge UP, 1999), that art can take on a new documentary power akin to what Camus also is attracted to in this component of his artistic self: *viz.* the capacity to capture the naked truth of things, not in their glorious appearances, but in their ignominious, usually passed over everydayness — what Benjamin called in a youthful essay of his own: "The elements of the ultimate condition [which] do not manifest themselves as formless progressive tendencies, but ... deeply rooted in the most endangered, excoriated, and ridiculed ideas and products ..." (Walter Benjamin, "The Life of Students", *Selected Writings Volume I* ed. Marcus Bullock, (USA: Belknap Press, 2004), p. 37.

[44] Albert Camus, "Art in Communion", in *Youthful Writings*, 222.

[45] Albert Camus, "Create Dangerously," in Resistance, Rebellion, Death trans. Justin O'Brien. (New York: Vintage, 1960), 259.

[46] Albert Camus, "The Enigma," *Lyrical and Critical Essays*, 158.

[47] Camus at Arthur Scherr, "Marie Cardona. An Ambivalent Nature-Symbol in Albert Camus's L'étranger" *Orbis Litterarum*, vol. 66, no. 1 (Feb. 2011), 12.

Srigley) have shown, Camus's *oeuvre* is littered with classical and biblical motifs which Camus arrays before contemporary audiences, and through which he frames his thoughts and narratives: Sisyphus, Oedipus, Prometheus, Don Juan, Cain, Christ, Adam and the fall, Demeter and Persephone, Orpheus, Faust and Nemesis.[49]

The point, which will lead us back to our considerations concerning Camus's Meursault and Caligula, is that this second strand of Camus's creative persona implies a quite different, much more prescriptive selection of elements and characters from the flow of experience than the minimal "absurd creation" celebrated in *The Myth of Sisyphus*. Mythological characters and narratives, however they are interpreted, are generally recognised to have some symbolic as well as a literal signification. This symbolic signification, moreover, is held in some manner to put the *mythoi* into communication with the deepest, perhaps archetypal, concerns and dimensions of human experience: those with which philosophy also is concerned. There are thus myths of cosmological origins, myths concerning death and the afterlife, the nature and origins of the soul; as well as myths in which exemplary heroic or divine characters present modes of conduct which we are asked to admire, if not to emulate. Greek mythology was the world in which he felt "most at ease," Camus famously commented.[50] Crochet has shown, by looking at the *Carnets*, that Camus's interest in *mythopoiesis* as an artistic vocation emerges at a precise, decisive point in his career: 1937-1938. Indeed, Camus was clearly attracted, via Spengler who he was reading at this time, to the thought that mythical narratives unfold outside of the ordinary order of historical time: involving what he termed "a denial of time of the strongest intensity."[51] What

---

[48] Cf. Jonathan Degenève, "« Quelle absence ! » : Blanchot lecteur de Camus," *Espace Maurice Blanchot*, at www-site http://www.blanchot.fr/fr/index.php?option=com_content&task=view&id=134&Itemid=41, last accessed July 16 2014. Cf. Maurice Blanchot, "De Dostoïevski à Kafka", in *L'Ere du soupçon*, (Paris: Gallimard, 1956, coll. « Folio Essais », 1987), p. 27.

[49] Monique Crochet (1973), Srigley (2010), also Walker (1982).

[50] Albert Camus, *Carnets II Janvier 1942 – Mars 1951*(Paris: Gallimard, 1964), 214.

[51] Camus at Monique Crochet, *Les Mythes*, 49. Cf. Camus's laconic "Absence du sens historique chez les Grecs » in the *Carnets* at Albert Camus, *Carnets I Mai 1935 – Février 1942* (Paris: Gallimard, 1962), 100.

seems to be involved here is simply the sense that a characterisation or action has mythical force to the extent that it addresses issues eternally recurrent for human beings (generational or sexual difference, political relations, suffering or death ...) and does so by presenting possible responses to these fundamental issues, which new generations still must confront, take up or reject.[52]. Mythical art for Camus, as we might say, is a living affront to the historicist view he assigns to Hegel (and which he sees as underlying the fascist and Stalinist ideologies) that human beings of any given time and culture are wholly the products of their historical times.[53]

It is characteristic of Camus — always a thinker of ambiguity or two-sidedness, *envers et endroit*[54] — that he tries to bring together these two (*témoignage* and myth-making) conceptions of artistic creation in his literary creation. Consider, for instance, the two sides of *The Plague*'s unusual formal profile. On the one hand, the book was criticised as a fairly transparent, almost mythical allegory of the Nazi occupation, and comment on the larger human condition.[55] Yet, allegories typically eschew any pretence to naturalism or realism. *The Plague*'s other formal side however is just such a presentation, as a realistic chronicle compiled from the sober testimony of the medically trained observer, Doctor Rieux. The reason Camus gives for his profound admiration for Melville's *Moby Dick* in this light is highly significant, since it indicates the type of balance between

---

[52] Cf. Crochet (1973), 44 on the decisive role of Spengler in shaping Camus's reception of classical mythology, and his notion that Greek mythology stages not the past, but timelessly recurrent patterns of the present: "in the same way that the history of Alexander the Great was confounded in antique sentiment with the legend of Dionysus even before his death ..." (Spengler at Crochet, *Les Mythes dans L'oeuvrre d'Albert Camus*, 44).

[53] On Camus's opposition to historicism, cf. Albert Camus, *Albert Camus Oeuvres Complètes II 1944-1948*741; 751; "Helen's Exile", *Lyrical and Critical Essays*, 150-1; also *L'Homme Révolté*, "Les "La Prophétie bourgeoise", 240-249.

[54] Cf. eg and esp. Albert Camus, *L'Homme Révolté*, 367-371; "Return to Tipasa", *Lyrical and Critical Essays*, 162-171.

[55] Cf. Camus at E. Freeman, *The Theatre of Albert Camus* (London: Methuen & Co., 1971), 84: "I want to express through the medium of the plague the suffocation from which we have all suffered and the atmosphere of menace and exile with which we have all lived. I want at the same time to extend this interpretation to the notion of existence in general. The plague will give the image of those in this war who have had the part of reflection, of silence — and that of moral suffering..."

descriptive testimony and myth-creation to which he aspired, and which this piece assigns to all great art. If Melville is great, says Camus, it is because, "like all great artists, constructed his symbols from the concrete, not in the material of dream ... inscribing them in the density [*épaisseur*] of reality and not in the fugitive clouds of the imagination."[56]

It is against this ideal of an art that balances objective descriptive sensitivity to the particularities of human experience, and the creation of mythical actions and characters that we think Camus's literary "absurd" should also be measured. Camus as an artist continued to experiment with trying to achieve this kind of balance between testimony and mythology, and we can see different manifestations of this, in their different genres, in *Caligula* and *The Stranger*. It is in this regard that Sartre's highly astute remarks on Meursault's mode of relating his "fate" in *L'Étranger* must be seen as giving us only one side of the story. In *The Stranger*, Sartre remarks:

> [E]ach sentence is an instant ... the sentences are not, of course, arranged in relation to each other; they are simply juxtaposed. In particular, all causal links are avoided lest they introduce the germ of an explanation and an order other than that of pure succession ..."[57]

Indeed, Meursault's testimony reflects his own almost indifferently floating attention to the succession of different moments in time, just as Sartre describes: "each sentence is a present instant .... Sharp, distinct and self-contained. It is separated by a void from the following one ... the world is destroyed and reborn from sentence to sentence."[58] Yet there is another side to this sense of a breakdown of linear, continuous time. The blank impersonal punctuality of Meursault's testimony, together with Camus's frequent scrambling of any sense of linear, unfolding time in the story, especially in the culminating beach scene, and Meursault's everywhere uncanny

---

[56] Cited at Crochet *Le Mythes*, 215; in translation, at Albert Camus, "On Herman Melville", in *Lyrical and Critical Essays*, 293. On Melville as creator of myths, cf. Albert Camus, "On Herman Melville", 289-293 inclusive.

[57] Jean-Paul Sartre, "Camus' *The Outsider*", 39, cf. 36-39.

[58] Jean-Paul Sartre, "Camus' *The Outsider*", 38.

impassivity or indifference — all this, together with Sartre's absence of any proffered explanatory principle, nevertheless conspire in the mind of the reader to produce exactly something like the ancient sense of "hazard" or fate central to Greek mythology and tragedy.[59] It is after all exactly such a sense of fatality that Meursault famously avows after he has fired his four shots into the unmoving arab's body on the beach, and which again strikes him as he watches the prosecutor, judge and defence discuss his deeds as the trial unfolds, and realises "for the first time" — as unwitting almost as Oedipus — "that I was guilty."[60]   Crochet has shown the extent to which *L'Étranger* can be seen to have drawn from, and adapted, mythological motifs from the biblical fall story, the scapegoating of Christ, and the tragedy of Oedipus.[61]   The role of a mythical transformation of, this time an historical story, is even clearer in *Caligula*. Camus himself stated concerning *Caligula* that although he drew the historical episodes the play's action recounts after Caligula's confrontation with the death of his sister-lover Drusilla from Suetonius, the play's presentation of Caligula, and interpretation of his motives and significance, was nevertheless all Camus's own: "nothing here is unhistorical.   The words are authentic, their exploitation is not."[62]

In this light, our point is, any assessment of what Meursault and Caligula are doing in Camus's *oeuvre,* relative to the wider movement of his developing thought, cannot rest with asserting the aesthetic autonomy, or purely descriptive neutrality of these works of art. The mythopoetic dimension to Camus's "absurd creations" means we must look to situate their action in the terms of what Camus's philosophical thought tells us are the fundamental parameters of

---

[59] One feature of epics and mythical is the way that they recount episodes in succession (say, the cycle of labours of Hercules), but often suppress or simply leave unexplained narrative connections between these episodes, almost like what Freud describes as "secondary revision" in the dream-work.

[60] Albert Camus, *The Stranger* translated by Stuart Gilbert (New York: Vintage Books, 1946), 55.

[61] Monique Crochet, *Les Mythes dans L'Oeuvre d'Albert Camus,* 129-133, 139-146.

[62] At Luke Richardson, "Sisyphus and Caesar: the Opposition of Greece and Rome in Albert Camus' Absurd Cycle," *Classical Receptions Journal,* Volume 4, Issue 1 (2012), 72.

human experience responded to in myth—albeit a thought now explored in literature that:

> ... ceasing to be renunciatory, flowers in images. It frolics — in myths, to be sure, but myths with no other depth than that of human suffering and, like it, inexhaustible. Not the divine fable that amuses and blinds, but the terrestrial face, gesture, and drama in which are summed up a difficult wisdom and an ephemeral passion ...[63]

2. Meursault and Caligula "avec Sade"

While we should honour the defence of *L'Étranger*'s relative autonomy from *Le Mythe de Sisyphe* proposed by Lamb and others, that is, we cannot wholly accede to it. It goes too far or, as Camus might put it, it is excessive, when a balance is needed. To put our contention differently again: we should not throw out the philosophical baby with the literary bathwater, at the same time as we resist seeing the novel (or Camus's plays) as thesis-like "illustrations" of the "philosophy of the absurd" and its allegedly amoral ethics. *L'Étranger*, Camus could reflect in his *Carnets*, "describes the nudity of man in face of the absurd."[64] There is also surely a good deal of Camus, and of those Algerians marooned outside of history he describes in "Summer in Algiers," in this Meursault. In an interview, Camus would thus chide his European interlocutor that in some sense Europeans would always be at a disadvantage in understanding his laconic anti-hero.[65] Moreover, Solomon seems right to us when he claims that Meursault's cathartic *anagnorēsis* and refusal of the metaphysical "escape" proffered him by the Priest in the novel's famous culminating action is unmistakably close to that "divine availability of the condemned man before whom the prison doors open in a certain early dawn" in

---

[63] Albert Camus, *Le Mythe de Sisyphe*, 158.

[64] Albert Camus, *Carnets II*, 36; Monique Crochet, *Les Mythes*, 133.

[65] Cf. Albert Camus, "Summer in Algiers", in *Lyrical and Critical Essays*, esp. 86: "and you understand that he is born in a land where everything is given to be taken away. In such abundance and profusion, ... reflection or self-improvement are quite irrelevant."

whom Camus affirms, in his own name, "the only reasonable freedom" in *Le Mythe*.[66] The reader of Camus's philosophical essay cannot be struck, when he turns to *Caligula* that other of the "absurd", by Caligula's anguished embroilment with several of the celebrated themes Camus analyses in *Le Mythe*: notably the imperial freedom of the man who has Révolté against all consoling myths and the "divine equivalence" of all things seen outside of societies' traditional evaluative categories.[67]

Whichever way we frame things, that is, Meursault and Caligula unmistakably embody different dramatic *responses* to "the absurd sensitivity which can be found widespread in the age," to which *Le Mythe* also responded.[68] This is one reason, together with the power of Camus's philosophical diagnosis of the dilemmas facing human beings living "beyond grace," underlying the unmistakably mythical register and fasciation of both texts. As such, the responses of Meursault to the death of *maman* and Caligula's traumatic acknowledgement that "people die, and are not happy"[69] are meant to have more than a particular, descriptive significance. Instead they are supposed to embody, like Ahab in *Moby Dick* or Alyosha, Dmitri and Ivan in *The Brothers Karamazov*, something like mythical figures embodying permanently available "tendencies or temptations" that face us all, insofar as we are faced with the absurd. The trick is to understand which *kinds* of responses to the absurd they embody, and in particular to challenge the too-facile assumption that must for Camus represent ideals to emulate or follow.

The question at this mythopoetic level is whether Meursault and Caligula, both of whom are (notably, given *The Rebel*) murderers represent "absurd heroes" or "saints of the absurd", for Camus?[70]

---

[66] Albert Camus, *Le Mythe*, 85.

[67] Cf. Albert Camus, *Le Mythe*, 75, 87-88, 96-97. Caligula's edifying theatrics are in part dedicated, he tells us, to making others understand truly what "freedom without frontier" (Albert Camus, "Caligula", 45) could involve, as the one free man in Rome ("Caligula," 48, 49).

[68] Albert Camus, *Le Mythe*, 16.

[69] Albert Camus, "Caligula", 40.

[70] This result would presumably go a long way to compromising Camus's philosophy, let alone his credentials as a moralist, whence its importance and recurrence.

Our thesis, at this point, is a simple *no*. Our argument here is that both Meursault's and Caligula's careers in these works represent less the kinds of positions Camus himself wants to advocate on the basis of an acknowledgement of the absurd than forms of that kind of "suicide" *The Myth of Sisyphus* both comprehends but advocates against. Confronting the absurd divorce between our hopes and comprehension and reality, Camus after all insists, is only a beginning — and its mere confrontation in no way prevents, indeed it can encourage us, as soon as possible to flee the "absurd deserts" back in to one or other form of metaphysical consolation, or the thoughtless rounds of habit.[71]

In fact, as Heffernan has shown, Camus can be seen to have placed many cues to alert us to how the hero of *The Outsider*, at least until his final awakening, represents nothing like Camus's ethical ideal or ideals, depicted in the second half of *Le Mythe* on the "absurd man".[72] As we glimpsed above in *Le Mythe*'s comments on the artistic life, Camus's ethical ideal is a kind of wakeful attentiveness to experience: if not the best living, then the most living: Meursault from beginning to near the end of *L'Étranger* is wracked by drowsiness, and periodic lapsings into sleep. When he is asked at trial concerning his motives, "I replied that I had pretty much lost the habit of analyzing myself": far from that "constant awareness, ever revived, ever alert" that impresses Camus most.

Most of all, however, until the very end of *L'Étranger*, Meursault is presented by Camus as less someone who soberly weighs nature's sovereign indifference to human purposes — embodied in the novel in the ever-present North African sun — while balancing this indifference against an appreciation of the human desire for unity and sense *than someone who is in effect more and more violently overcome by nonhuman nature*. It is with light, above all, that Meursault has particular difficulties. In the novel's opening pages, it is "the glare of light" off the road and from the sky that makes Meursault want to sleep on the bus to *maman*'s home.[73] The glare from the walls of the

---

[71] Cf. Albert Camus, *Le Mythe*, 48-74 ("Le Suicide Philosophique").

[72] I am indebted greatly to George Heffernan, "Mais personne ne parraissait comprendre": Athiesm, Nihilism, and Hermeneutics in Albert Camus' *L'Étranger/The Stranger Analecta Husserliana* CIX (2011), 133–152,

"bright, spotlessly keen" mortuary, and its white walls[74], leads Meursault to ask his hosts if they cannot turn the lights down — in response to which, he is told that no, they are 'all or nothing'.[75] When maman's friends arrive, and Meursault is awoken:

> I had a feeling that the light had grown even stronger than before .... Never in my life had I seen anyone as clearly as I say these people: not a detail of their clothes or features escaped me."[76]

At *maman*'s funeral, again, the sky is described by Meursault as "a blaze of light," or a furnace with "the air stoking up rapidly ... "[77] so as to threaten to obliterate all possibility of human inhabitancy: "now, in the full glare of the morning sun, with everything shimmering in the heat haze, there was something inhuman, discouraging, about this landscape."[78] Things famously culminate, however, in the dreadful moment of the murder. Camus's narration makes it clear that, at this fateful moment, Meursault is veritably assaulted by "the same sun as at *maman*'s funeral"; blinded to all human significance in the murderous epiphany of the sun:

> A shaft of light shot upward from the steel, and I felt as if a long, thin blade transfixed my forehead. At the same moment all the sweat that had accumulated in my eyebrows splashed down on my eyelids, covering them with a warm film of moisture. Beneath a veil of brine and tears my eyes were blinded; I was conscious only of the cymbals of the sun clashing on my skull, and, less distinctly, of the keen blade of light flashing up from the knife,

---

[73] Albert Camus, *The Stranger*, 4.

[74] Albert Camus, *The Stranger*, 6, 7.

[75] Albert Camus, *Stranger*, 7. This is a significant phrase for Camus, especially in *The Rebel*, where it comes to delineate the kinds of excessive, finally murder-vindicating thinking he associates with totality and revolution, in contrast to unity and rebellion.

[76] Albert Camus, *Stranger*, 8.

[77] Albert Camus, Stranger, 11. We note that the sand under their feet stokes up on the day of the murder (*Stranger* 33), it was hot like a furnace on the beach (*Stranger* 36), and that the sky is starting to "stoke up" again at exactly the time of day when Meursault's trial properly begins, at *Stranger*, 54.

[78] Albert Camus, *Stranger*, 11.

> scarring my eyelashes, and gouging into my eyeballs. Then
> everything began to reel before my eyes, a fiery gust came
> from the sea, while the sky cracked in two, from end to end,
> and a great sheet of flame poured down through the rift.
> Every nerve in my body was a steel spring, and my grip
> closed on the revolver. The trigger gave, and the smooth
> underbelly of the butt jogged my palm. And so, with that
> crisp, whipcrack sound, it all began ...[79]

Meursault, until at least his closing catharsis, thus represents anything but a Camusian ideal attesting to kind of lucid, wakeful confrontation between human desire and the inhumanity of the world the author of *Le Mythe de Sisyphe* celebrates. He is in fact, until his final cathartic confrontation with the Priest, someone increasingly passively overwhelmed by this inhumanity, until he becomes almost its murderous avatar. It is because of the sun that he killed, so he testifies, but no one listens.[80] "Suicide" may not be right word here: since it implies a sense of volition that Meursault vividly attests to having lost, and after the shooting he is more or less constrained by the state, watching on with curious fascination as the state tries and decides to kill him. Thinking forward to Camus's typology of responses to the existence of senseless suffering in *The Rebel*, we want now to suggest, this fatal blindness comes closest to anticipating the kind of "absolute negation" Camus ascribes to the romantics and the Marquis de Sade.

To make this claim, we need therefore to briefly recall how Camus delineates these kinds of "figures of spirit" in *L'Homme Révolté*, whose representatives (like Meursault in *L'Étranger*) end up with blood on their hands. For Camus, what marks off these figures' "metaphysical rebellion" against the idea of a providential, salvific God is their sense that the reality of evil represents proof positive that God's order is inhumane. While Camus's rebel also accepts this modern notion, what singles out Sade and the romantics is that they "leap" from acknowledging the reality of such divinely or naturally-

---

[79] Albert Camus, *Stranger* 38-39.

[80] Camus, *The Stranger*, 64: "I tried to explain that it was because of the sun, but I spoke too quickly and ran my words into each other. I was only too conscious that it sounded nonsensical, and, in fact, I heard people tittering ..."

ratified evil, to citing this evil as justification for their own literary celebrations of transgression against this order as ends in themselves. "In order to combat evil, the rebel renounces good, because he considers himself innocent, and once again gives birth to evil,"[81] Camus argues concerning these figures: from Milton, then Vigny and Lermontov's sympathy with the devil, through to Lermontov's Maldador, whose copulations with a shark and attack on the Creator Himself in the form of an octopus are "are clear expressions of an escape beyond the frontiers of existence and of a convulsive attack on the laws of nature."[82]

The Prince amongst these "men of letters", however, is Sade. Sade does not propose attacking the unjust Deity: far from it. As Jacques Lacan discerned a little after Camus (with common reference to Klossowski's *Sade, mon prochain*)[83], having surmised that God must have willed senseless human suffering, Sade instead sides with this evil big Other, as the only effectively pious thing to do.[84] The fortresses of crime he thus established have more of the convent about them than only their segregation from the profane world wherein men give way, without rhyme or reason, on their untethered desires. Sade's for instance stipulates that all the *jouisseurs* should periodically confess concerning the exactions and infamies.[85] These "strongholds of debauchery where a kind of bureaucracy of vice rules over the life and death"[86] are engaged in the business of doing God's work, or the work of Nature, carrying out the violent edicts of the inhuman natural order: "a lawless universe where the only master is the inordinate energy of desire."[87] To be true to this

---

[81] Camus, *L'Homme Révolté*, 71.

[82] Camus, *L'Homme Révolté*, 114.

[83] Cf. Camus, *L'Homme Révolté*, 61.

[84] Compare Jacques Lacan, "Kant With Sade": "Sade ... stopped at the point where desire and the law became bound up with each other [*se noue*]. / If something in him lets itself remain tied to the law in order to take the opportunity, mentioned by Saint Paul, to become inordinately sinful, who would cast the first stone? But Sade went no further./ It is not simply that the flesh is weak, as it is for each of us; it is that the spirit is not willing not to be deluded. [Sade's] apology for crime merely impels him to an oblique acceptance of the Law. The Supreme Being [as for instance the Nature of Pius VI] is restored in Evil Action [*le Maléfice*]," at 667 [Fr. 790]).

[85] Camus, *L'Homme Révolté*, 65.

[86] Camus, *L'Homme Révolté*, 64.

libidinal order, we are called upon to give up on all our merely whimsical pleasures—in an ironic or demonic doubling of Kant's purely deontological ethics, as Lacan, Adorno and Horkheimer[88] each maintained:

> It is a curious kind of pleasure, no doubt, which obeys the commandment: 'We shall rise every morning at ten o'clock'! But enjoyment must be prevented from degenerating into attachment, it must be put in parentheses and toughened. Objects of enjoyment must also never be allowed to appear as persons. If man is 'an absolutely material species of plant,' he can only be treated as an object and as an object for experiment. In Sade's fortress republic, there are only machines and mechanics.[89]

In Camus's *Caligula*, the proximity between Camus's absurd anti-hero and this Sadean position is more direct than in the ambivalent case of Meursault. Like Sade, with whose clear-sighted apprehension that "murder is an attribute of the divinity", Camus agrees[90], Caligula's eyes are opened by Drusilla's death to the reality "that nothing lasts,"[91] including human lives, despite the fact that ordinary social conventions seem to conspire to conceal or avoid acknowledging this larger reality of our condition. Thus is explained the emperor's "devastating scorn"[92] for all social convention, and the desires of others for wealth, status, power, love, recognition, or comfort. He declaims, as Meursault still does at the end, "everything's on an equal footing"[93], "the world has no importance ..."[94]; "it all comes to the same in the end."[95] But, like the romantics, here again Caligula's rebellion against this unhappy fate flips almost

---

[87] Camus, *L'Homme Révolté*, 60.
[88] Cf. Adorno and Horkeimer, "Excursus II: Juliette, or the Enlightenment and Morals".
[89] Camus, *L'Homme Révolté*, 65.
[90] Camus, *L'Homme Révolté*, 59.
[91] Camus, "Caligula", 102, cf. 101.
[92] Camus, "Caligula," 69, 102.
[93] Camus, "Caligula," 43-44.
[94] Camus, "Caligula," 46. Cf. Camus, *Stranger*, 74.
[95] Camus, "Caligula," 64.

immediately to the perverse, "logical" conclusion that the only thing left to do, condemned as we are to this order, is to consciously *oneself* take on the violences of which we are otherwise merely the passive victims. Hence, far from rejecting the irrationality and inhumanity of the world that provokes his rebellion, Caligula 'sides with' this irrationality, no less than Camus depicts Shestov or Kierkegaard doing in the realm of ideas. It is just that Caligula then — here more like a kind of murderous dandy, and as good as his words — sets about making an example of himself: using his absolute power as a kind of pedagogical theatre[96] or classroom to open the eyes of his contemporaries to their fate. By the same murderous token, Caligula tells us, "to prove to the imaginary gods that any man, without prior training, can play their absurd role to perfection ... all that's needed is to be as cruel as they."[97] Caligula, as he says, "plays the part of Fate"[98] and natural or divine evil, just as Sade had dreamed for his libertines: "it's I who replace the epidemics ..."[99]

And the result, once more, is not a life well lived, lucid before the absurd and faithful to each of its competing demands. It is a murderous career that culminates in Caligula salving his immovable sense of guilt by consenting to his own death at the hands of Cherea and his bands of partisans.[100] To paraphrase Camus's summation of Kierkegaard's and Shestov's "existential philosophies": in Meursault standing on the beach with a gun in his hand, and Caligula declaiming on the need for a Great Transformation, we see that "all without exception suggest escape."[101]

Concluding Remarks

The argumentative work in this paper is now done. We have tried to steer a middle course between the position represented pre-

---

[96] Cf. Camus, "Caligula," 49.
[97] Camus, "Caligula," 74-75.
[98] Camus, "Caligula," 92.
[99] Camus, "Caligula," 92, cf. 75.
[100] Camus, "Caligula," 104, cf. 78-85 where Caligula's suicidal desire to be killed by the resistants is made clear.
[101] Camus, *Le Mythe*, 52.

eminently by Sartre, according to which Camus's early fiction "illustrate" the absurd, and the position of figures like Lamb who want to deny any link between Camus's philosophical reflection in *The Myth of Sisyphus* and the two literary "absurds."[102] Returning to Camus's ongoing reflections on aesthetics and his own artistic practices, we argued that there is an entire, important dimension of Camus's artistic persona—as a creator of myths aimed to speak to contemporary men and women, and the difficulties we face living after the contestation of the West's "sacred canopy"—whose existence prompts us to posit *some* relation between the philosophical discourses and the characters and actions staged in Camus's fictions. The golden thread we followed comes in Camus's important remark concerning Roger Martin du Gard, that artists' characters may not directly represent themselves so much as "tendencies and temptations" s/he has herself experienced. *The Myth of Sisyphus* and *The Rebel* both document that confronting the absurd (in *Le Mythe*) or the reality of natural and human evil (in *L'Homme Révolté*) involve temptations to "leap" into one or other form of "all or nothing" position—positing that all *must* be rational, despite contrary evidence; or that the evident *irrationality* of the world is itself the True and Final word. In this light, it becomes possible (and arguably closest to Camus's own intentions) to maintain both that the literary "absurds" are not "completely independent" of the philosophical discourse of *Le Mythe de Sisyphe*, while denying that either Meursault nor Caligula in Camus's early, ground-breaking fiction represent exemplary ethical responses to the disjunction between human hopes and what the world provides. Each encounters the absurd, and aspects of their characters and actions—the observant, present-minded lucidity in Meursault, and Caligula's distance from conventional values and concerns—resonate with aspects of Camus's ethics in *The Myth of Sisyphus* and *The Rebel*. Yet Camus is always clear that fidelity to the absurd requires a lucid openness to all aspects of experience as they present themselves, and the ethical imperative to preserve the conscious human lives (one's own in *L Mythe*, and those of others, in *The Rebel*) that can maintain this awareness. Yet both *The Stranger* and *Caligula* document the stories

---

[102] Cf. Albert Camus, *Carnets I Mai 1935-Février 1942*, 224.

of murderers: in Meursault's case, that of an almost unwitting killer, overwhelmed by the intrusive heat and light of the North African sun; but in Caligula's case, with the same kind of philosophical self-awareness that characterises Sade's dilettantes, whom Caligula's theatrical actions and monologues sometimes call to mind. In the light of the philosophical perspective Camus develops from *Le Mythe* into *The Rebel*, each of these figures embodies a form of absolute negation or irrationalism: as it were, passively or actively "siding with" the inhuman dimensions of the world, whose plagues, natural disasters and encroaching transience challenge humans' best efforts to create unity and meaning from their condition. Although we do not have the space to explore this here, it should also be underlined that neither anti-hero exhausts the range of options of responding to the absurd that each text stages. Camus tells us that he always remained most fond of Marie and Céleste of all his characters in *L'Étranger*[103], and there are moments of sympathy in the text also for Salamano and his dog[104]; whereas Caligula's madness is soon discerned, and then overcome, by Cherea, whose resistance to Caligula's tyranny, moved by the desire "to regain peace of mind in a world that has regained a meaning" or "… to live, and to be happy" much more closely approach what we know Camus's own biographical course to have been.[105] Meursault and Caligula, that is, are to be read "with Sade," to evoke once more Jacques Lacan's famously provocative title aligning the Marquis with Immanuel Kant. Their tales are not "absurd heroes" but mythopoetic, literary explorations of the all-too-human ways that, unable to bear the absurd and its exigencies, human beings seek to elude or escape their finitude, much too often by visiting this finitude upon others.

---

[103] Albert Camus, "Three Interviews,", *Lyrical and Critical Essays*, 361.
[104] Cf. Ingrid Fernandez, "Of Dogs and Men: Empathy and Emotion in Camus' *The Stranger*" *Journal of Camus Studies* (2012), 53-56.
[105] Albert Camus, "Caligula," 54-82.

REVIEW: FRANCOFONIA 65 – CAMUS/PASOLINI: DEUX ÉCRIVAINS "ENGAGÉS"

by Giovanni Gaetani

2013 was without any doubt, a great, memorable year for all the readers and specialists of Albert Camus's works. Indeed, on occasion of his birth centenary many remarkable events took place worldwide – conferences, expositions, publications, and documentaries. One of these events is the publication of the issue 65 of *Francofonia* on *Camus/Pasolini: deux écrivains "engagés"*, edited under the guide of Silvia Disegni, professor of French Literature at the University of Naples "Federico II".

Founded in 1981 by Liano Petroni (1921-2006), who has been one of the most important Italian critics of Camus, as well as a close friend, *Francofonia* is a six-monthly journal of study and research on francophone literature, published under the auspices of the University of Bologna "Alma Mater Studiorum". This issue of the journal is a partial gathering of the texts presented at the homonymous international meeting held in Naples (15th-18th November 2010), well-described by Silvia Disegni in her introduction.

All along the nine texts – of which two in French and seven in Italian – the undeniable political, artistic, and philosophical affinities between Camus and Pasolini are analyzed. A study of the potential mutual influences is instead missing, both for a precise choice of the authors (p. 3 and p. 117) and for a matter of necessity: indeed, even if chronologically belonging to the same generation (Camus was born in 1913 while Pasolini in 1922), the two intellectuals unfortunately never had the opportunity to meet each other in real life. This *rencontre manquée* is even more absurd if we consider that Camus and Pasolini had many friends in common (Carlo Levi, Nicola Chiaromonte, Ignazio Silone) and some real opportunities to meet, as both Silvia Disegni and Samantha Novello show (pp. 15-16 and p. 92, note 41). Despite their distance in life, they actually share a certain intellectual approach to existence, a way to see and describe things, a particular attitude to art and, lastly, a common political sensibility.

In her essay *Camus/Pasolini: Posture ex-centrique de deux écrivains journalistes "engagés" du XXᵉ siècle*, Silvia Disegni masterfully shows us the similar ways in which Camus and Pasolini have been two eccentric journalists and writers: starting from their will to "think and live in our history" (Camus, p. 16), that is, "to not place themselves outside history" (Pasolini, p. 17), Disegni discusses how and why they both refused the notion of *engagement*, preferring to it the one of *témoignage*. In their perspectives the artist cannot follow the orders of a party, nor he can express the orthodox doctrines of a political view with his art, as already André Gide remarked in his important *Retour de l'U.R.S.S.*, a book who had a great impact on Camus. "One must not commit the error to reduce an art work to a mere political message", says Disegni, clarifying also that for Camus the relationship between art and politics is "tautological": "it is not the fight that makes us artists, it is the art that forces us to be fighters" (Camus, p. 19). There are, anyway, some extreme cases in which the artists must get out of his artistic universe in order to defend his ideas with other means – what the author rather calls *intervention*. Pasolini is illuminating at this regard (p. 21): 'in some occasions the artist must have the civil courage to stop expressing himself trough the mediation of his works and, then, to start expressing himself directly, with his own existence, that is, to "throw" his body into the fight'.

The essay goes on analyzing the peculiar position that both intellectuals occupy, the one of "the lonely knight, the Franc-tireur" that the author defines *ex-centrique* (p. 24), underling once more the Greek and Latin etymology of the term (ἔκκεντρος, *ex-centrum*, outside the center). After a close examination of the biographical and geographical reasons that clarify their eccentricity towards society and towards their respective communist parties (p. 25), the essay ends with a critical paragraph in which the author points out that too often both Camus and Pasolini rhetorically claimed their eccentricity as a kind of exclusion, when instead they were in fact publicly recognized from all their contemporary intellectual colleagues and, more in general, from the institutionalized intellectual *milieu* (pp. 27-30). Disegni concludes his work quoting Bourdieu, who defines the intellectual field as a "paradoxical universe in which freedom from institutions is found inscribed in those institutions" (p. 30).

Jeanyves Guérin, whose name cannot be unknown to every true Camus' specialist, being the editor of the fundamental *Dictionnaire Albert Camus*, gives us a perfect, detailed, and synthetic reconstruction of what he calls *Smarrimenti algerini di un "giusto"*. The text by Guérin, originally in French, has been translated to Italian by Michela Lo Feudo and Silvia Disegni with its title translated in English as: *Algerian losses of a "Just"*, evidently with reference to *Les Justes*. This text follows and recaps what Guérin has already written in many previous works on the subject (see note 23, p. 47): his main aim is to restore a certain objectivity on Camus' complex position towards Algeria's independence war, which at the moment remains the last true accusation addressed to Camus from every side of the critique. Indeed, as the author sadly ascertains in the opening of his essay: "Today three sentences still blur twenty-five years of Camusian writings", referring to the famous – but always badly reported – sentence of Camus "if this is justice, I prefer my mother" (*si c'est cela, la justice, je préfère ma mère*) (p. 33). Far from being an apologetic text or a kind of short pamphlet, this essay is instead a witness of Guerin's historical knowledge as well as of his intellectual honesty: in fact, while he recognizes Camus' courage and good faith in his request for a federal Algeria and an immediate civil truce, he points out also Camus' naivety and incapacity to analyze appropriately the geopolitical situation of French Algeria, given his generalizations and undervaluation of the Arab culture and his "gallo-centrica" (French-oriented) education (p. 41). In his conclusion Guerin regrets that today "we hear no voice like Camus' one": "His hesitations, his scruples, even his contradictions make him a person close to us, closer than his detractors, so stiffened in their certainties" (p. 47).

The essay of Riccardo Antoniani ("Oil, *the* Vas of *Italian political economy*" – "Vas" was an alternative title of the novel; it is an implicit reference to the biblical expression *vas electionis*, from the *Acts of Apostles* 9, 15) focuses on Pasolini's unfinished novel *Petrolio* (Oil), which is considered by the author a key-text to understand Italy's real economical and political situation in 1960s and 1970s (p. 53): 'moving the horizon of his analysis towards political economy Pasolini understood in advance that the gap between economy and politics was progressively decreasing in favour of economy and of its new productive cycles'.

With an excellent, precise historical knowledge, fruit also of the oral witnesses gathered by Antoniani himself (see notes 15, 53, 55, 63), the author analyzes all the hidden circumstances that clearly connect this masterpiece of Pasolini with his mysterious assassination (p. 50-52). Remarkable is also the discussion of how Pasolini's image has been too often muddied and mocked by the Italian journalists of all periods, before and after the tragic death of the author, for reasons of pure political servility (pp. 54-57). Except for few passages where a too elaborate syntax does not help the comprehension, this essay of Antoniani is definitely a fundamental tool to understand *Petrolio*'s historical and political significance, as well as Pasolini's intellectual grandeur.

The work of Umberto Todini (*Antichità contro. Albert Camus e Pier Paolo Pasolini*, literally *Antiquities against...*) together with the one of Oreste Lippolis (*La forma del mito, i segni della storia nell'opera di Pier Paolo Pasolini*, that is, *The form of the myth, the signs of history in Pasolini's works*) and the one of Marco Antonio Bazzocchi (*Pasolini/Camus corpi nel deserto – Pasolini/Camus, bodies in the desert*) give us a detailed, interesting, and exhaustive survey of the literary relationship of the two authors with the ancient myths and characters, mainly from the Greek world: Camus with Sisyphus, Prometheus, Oedipus, Nemesis, and Caligula; Pasolini with Oedipus the King, Medea, the Oresteia, and many others non-mythological subjects (the Decameron, the Canterbury Tales, the Gospel of Matthew, etc.). The conclusive words of Todini can condense the meaning of Camus's and Pasolini's use of the ancient myth (p. 76): 'With Camus and Pasolini [...] the ancients start to come off from their pedestals where they were placed for centuries, in order to show themselves for what they actually are, self-critical, Brechtianly alienating ("brechtianamente stranianti"), within our means ("alla portata"). The cultural, academic, bookish, celluloid power of such models of classicalities must face a principle of reality that lets emerge differently ancient and differently modern men ("uomini diversamente antichi e diversamente moderni")'.

Samantha Novello is at the moment one of the most important Italian critics of Camus – indeed, she is the only Italian scholar that worked at the four tomes edition of Camus' complete works, edited by Gallimard. Her precious essay, *Il rovescio e il diritto. Il pensiero politico di Albert Camus fra tragedia antica e tragico moderno* (*The right side and the wrong side. The political thought of Albert Camus between ancient tragedy and the modern one*), exposes with great accuracy and elegance Camus' position towards modern nihilism, its spiritual disguises and its political degenerations. Analyzing Nietzsche's and Scheler's key influence concerning Camus' understanding of the concept of *ressentiment* (resentment towards reality and men, both conceived as "morally negative", p. 80 and p. 84) Novello shows us the way the absurd reflection of *The Myth of Sisyphus* tried to achieve a tragic but optimistic thought (p. 88), in which life is no longer expiation of a primordial, metaphysical sin, but rather "a vision of love, that transforms every curse ("*male*dizione") in a blessing ("*bene*dizione") and that denies the will to power" (p. 92). The variety and precision of all the bibliographical references are remarkable and definitely make this essay a valuable, praiseworthy analysis of the essential core of Camus' philosophical attempt.

The last two essays of this issue are the one of Hervé Joubert-Laurencin (*Entre Camus et Pasolini: Mastroianni, l'homme solaire, l'homme minéral*), who with originality and creativity analyzes the works of Pasolini and Camus through the figure of Marcello Mastroianni, a famous Italian actor who embodied both Meursault in Luchino Visconti's *The Stranger* and the protagonist of Mauro Bolognini's *Bell'Antonio*, whose screenwriter was just Pasolini; and the brief but thick essay of Filippo La Porta (*Vite parallele. Camus e Pasolini maestri irregolari*, that is, *Parallel lives. Camus and Pasolini irregular masters*) where the author describes separately the lives of the two intellectuals, in order to show their convergences of methods and of personalities, nonetheless respecting their essential diversities.

They share a certain loyalty to the present, because they are aware that "violence, power, and falsehood are born from the idea of future, of a remote justice, and of a calculation of what will happen" (p. 143); they share also a will to maintain a "radical connection between biography and thought" (p. 145). In La Porta's perspective, Pasolini's works express an "atheist and gnostic religiosity" (p. 146), while Camus is a "philosopher without method and system" (p. 148), "a big and troublesome amateur of thought" (p. 149). The conclusion of the author, though a little bit rhetorical, is rather efficacious and underlines once more the proximity of the two authors (p. 150): 'I like to imagine Camus and Pasolini playing in the same team, with different roles, in a dusty, suburban soccer field, under a dazzling, meridian sun' .

In conclusion, this issue of *Francofonia* is definitely an important and innovative contribution to both Camus's and Pasolini's studies. Though the circumstances of life kept them apart and though two tragic, premature deaths prevented them to finally meet, in this issue we can instead see the two intellectuals ideally talking each other. In this way, their *étrangeté* has eventually disappeared and their faces are more similar than ever before.

Camus/Pasolini deux écrivains "engagés" [Camus/Pasolini two writers "engaged"] is a special issue of *Francofonia* (issue 65). Edited by Silvia Disegni (2013).

MANUSCRIPT SUBMISSION GUIDELINES

Mission & Scope

The Journal of Camus Studies is an interdisciplinary forum for scholarly conversation about the life and work of Albert Camus. The goal of the Journal of Camus Studies is to provide a genuinely international and interdisciplinary scholarly resource for exploration and examination of the thought of Albert Camus and his contemporaries.

The *Journal of Camus Studies* was founded in 2008 as the *Journal of the Albert Camus Society* by Simon Lea. The inaugural volume represented the work of international authors exploring the life and work of Camus from a variety of philosophical and theoretical perspectives. In 2010, Peter Francev was appointed General Editor in an effort to focus more intentionally on reaching an academic audience.

Manuscripts

Abstracts: Prior to manuscript submission, authors are asked to submit the following: full contact information along with a brief, one-paragraph biography detailing current affiliation, research interests and recent publications, as well as an abstract of no more than 250 words.

Manuscript Preparation: Manuscripts should be no longer than 10,000 words (text and notes). The entire paper must be double-spaced, with one-inch margins and 12-point font, in MS Word. Both the paper and notes must conform to the *MLA Style Manual and Guide to Scholarly Publishing*, 3rd edition. They must avoid sexist and ethnic biases. Also, manuscripts must not be under consideration by another publication. Along with the manuscript, the author must prepare a separate file as a cover letter. This file will include a history of the manuscript, whether it is derived from an M.A. or Ph.D. thesis with the advisor's name, whether it has been presented at a conference, or other pertinent information about its development. Authors are encouraged to submit all materials using MS Word to the General Editor who, then, will forward the materials to the review committee.

Review Process

The *Journal of Camus Studies* follows a policy of blind, peer review; please ensure that the main body of the manuscript contains no identifying remarks. All comments by reviewers are confidential and shall not be published. Final judgment with regard to publication is made by the General Editor.

When the editor receives a submission, the manuscript will undergo a peer review. At least, two reviewers will provide evaluative comments for each submission. On the basis of this review, the manuscript may be unconditionally rejected, conditionally accepted, or unconditionally accepted for publication. Each submitter will be provided with the peer review statements and may respond to the comments, ask questions, or seek clarification as desired. Evaluations, typically, will be complete within 6-8 weeks. Standard evaluation forms are used by the reviewers. If a particular reviewer cannot complete a review within a timely manner, the editor will seek an alternative, qualified reviewer. Sometimes the opinion of a reviewer is important enough that the editor must wait a little longer.

Conference Announcements

Announcements and correspondence regarding conferences, panels, papers, and other news of interest should be sent to the Editor, *Journal of Camus Studies*, at the following address:

Professor Peter Francev
General Editor, *Journal of Camus Studies*
Dept. of English
Mount San Antonio College
1100 N. Grand Ave
Walnut, California 91789-1399

pfrancev@mtsac.edu

Book Reviews

Book Review Preparation: Book Reviews should be a minimum of 750 words and no longer than 2,500 words. The entire review must be double-spaced, with one-inch margins and 12-point font, in MS Word. The review must conform to the MLA Style Manual and Guide to Scholarly Publishing, 3rd edition, or The Chicago Manual of Style, 15th edition. They must avoid sexist and ethnic biases, be written in English. Reviews must not be under consideration by another publication. The conclusion of the review should state the author's name and affiliation or current city, state, and country of residence.

Upon receipt of submission, the Book Review Editor will conduct an initial review to determine that the review is suitable for publication in the Journal. The Book Review Editor may then decline to pass the manuscript on for publication. The Editor and Associate Editors always seek to find the most qualified reviewers to evaluate books.

Deadline: Submission deadline: 30th September of each year. This allows the Editors ample time to review submissions, and still permit for revisions prior to publication.

Books to be Reviewed: Books relevant to the life and times of Albert Camus should be sent to the Book Review Editor, *Journal of Camus Studies*, at the following address:

Eric B. Berg
Book Review Editor, *Journal of Camus Studies*
Associate Professor of Philosophy
MacMurray College
447 East College Avenue
Jacksonville, IL 62650

Books sent from within the UK should be sent to:

BM Camus Mail,
London WC1N 3XX